S0-ADT-927

AN ANTHOLOGY
of
PURE POETRY

AN ANTHOLOGY
of
PURE POETRY

EDITED WITH AN INTRODUCTION
BY
GEORGE MOORE

LIVERIGHT NEW YORK

Copyright © 1924 by Boni & Liveright, Inc.
Copyright renewed 1952 by C. D. Medley.
All rights reserved. No part of this book
may be reproduced in any form without
permission in writing from the publisher.

ISBN: 0-87140-083-9
Library of Congress Catalog Card Number: 72-96901

Liveright Paperbound Edition 1973

1.987654321

Manufactured in the United States of America

AN ANTHOLOGY
of
PURE POETRY

INTRODUCTION

I

ALTHOUGH deflowered thirty or forty years ago
in *Confessions of a Young Man,* the incident that
led me to poetry must be related here, so significant
does it seem to me to be of every man's adventures
among books.

When I was a child of nine, ten, or eleven, the
family coach, a coach hung upon Cee springs, came
round to the front door to take us to the County of
Galway, and as we had promised to arrive at Head-
fort in time for breakfast our start was an early one,
not later than half-past six or seven in the morning.
My father and mother lay back talking in a deep,
cushioned seat; and I remember envying them, for
I was seated with my brother on a hard bench, our
backs to the horses; and the swinging of the coach
and the shining of the sun through the glass on my
face caused a sickness to rise up in me. I was about
to ask my parents to lower the window-blind when
a kindly cloud veiled the sun, and it was at that
moment I heard my father telling my mother about
Lady Audley. Maurice was too young to be inter-
ested in a beautiful name and in the story of a woman
who ran away with her groom for he had violet

[9]

eyes, and my mother wishing to abandon herself un-
reservedly to the charm of hearing my father relate
the murder of the groom, begged me to keep quiet.
My father's words were more peremptory: Hold
your tongue, George! My resolution, however, was
taken to read the book as soon as we returned home.
Lady Audley's Secret led me to *John Marchmont's
Towers* and thence to *Aurora Floyd,* and from
Aurora Floyd I passed on to *The Doctor's Wife,* an
adaptation of *Madame Bovary* in which Miss Brad-
don retained only the country doctor and his wife,
a sentimentalised Emma, who found content, or
didn't, in Byron and Shelley. To the sound of Shel-
ley's name my grandfather's library was searched
for the poems and at last a short, thick volume in
red boards was discovered behind a line of books.
It contained a portrait of the poet, ringleted, pen-
sive, beautiful, goose quill in hand, and the fortune
of the volume being to open at *The Sensitive Plant,*
my imagination was so fanned by the description of
the garden that I could not do else than rush to my
mother's room to tell her of what I had found,
detaining her in her dressing. And so ardent was
my pleading for her hearing of some stanzas if not
the whole of the poem, that she agreed to listen,
but she soon put me out of her room through a
green baize door, saying: George, Georgie would
like to read you some poetry. My father, pleased
by my enthusiasm, for I was a backward child, ac-
cepted my admiration of *The Sensitive Plant,* and
to put me to what seemed to him a test more con-

[10]

clusive of intelligence, he took the book out of my hand and read the opening lines of *Queen Mab*. I asked him to read them a second time and then a third time, so that I might commit them to memory; and having repeated some three or four lines correctly I begged that the book should be given back to me, for I would read to him *The Pine Forest by the Sea*. He gave a hearing to about half the poem and then resumed his shaving, remarking, with a view to discouraging me with my poet, that he could not understand why I should take so much pleasure in reading bad verses. Yet he was not indifferent to poetry, and to persuade me to read better verses he recited the beautiful lines from *Christabel*:

> The night is chill; the forest bare;
> Is it the wind that moaneth bleak?
> There is not wind enough in the air
> To move away the ringlet curl
> From the lovely lady's cheek——

But it was not the lady's curl that moved me to cry: Father, how beautiful! but:

> The one red leaf, the last of its clan,
> That dances as often as dance it can,
> Hanging so light, and hanging so high,
> On the topmost twig that looks up at the sky.

Lines whose beauty never grows less but is increased perhaps by association with the moment when I heard them for the first time—my beloved father laying down his hair brushes, restoring the stoppers to the vials of macassar-oil and the top to the poma-tum pot.

And the sight of a name having discovered a great poet to me, I sought for another name betokening poetry. The name Kirke White seemed to herald a poet, although not so great a poet as the name Percy Bysshe Shelley; I am quite sure I did not place the same reliance on the name of Kirke White as I had done on the name of Percy Bysshe Shelley, but I did not doubt that it signified poetry, and the bookseller in Castlebar was written to many times, importuned till at last a letter came from him saying that he hoped to receive the book by the next post. The market cart went to Castlebar once a week, but my longing for Kirke White could not brook so long a delay; a special messenger was engaged by me to walk sixteen miles for the book; he started early— a shilling was the fare—and at five o'clock I was awaiting his arrival in the pantry, putting my father's valet past his patience with tiresome inquiries and excursions to the head of the kitchen stairs. At last the messenger's nailed shoes were heard on the stone stairs, but I did not give him time to reach the top. I called that the volume should be handed to me over the banisters, and snatching it, I fled with it to my room, bolting the door after me, so afraid was I of an interruption. But how shall I tell of the great sickness of heart that fell upon me, how I walked in despondency for the first time, my hope being, and it was only a very faint one, that I should discover a poet behind the name of Abraham Cow-

ley, the second string to my bow. . . . Byron pleased
me, but only fairly well. I liked the passages my
father pointed out to me and committed some pages
of *Sardanapalus* to memory out of deference to his
judgment, feeling, however, that they lacked, for me
at least, the spiritual ecstasy which at that time I
was so intent on finding, which I sought and found
in many poets, but in none so flagrantly as I did in
Shelley.

We often went to Castle Carra for picnics, and I
think it has been mentioned in some autobiographi-
cal works that the old gateway always excited my
mother to recite a passage from *Marmion*. The de-
scent of the portcullis as Marmion galloped through,
shearing away a plume from his crest, annoyed me,
but I was obliged to refrain from criticism, for I was
without power to translate my feelings into words.
I was often reluctant to listen to my father reading
The Lay of the Last Minstrel; in truth I liked it no
better than *Marmion* and detested the volume of
Burke's speeches which he urged me to read in the
billiard room. But this, too, has been related in
one of the volumes of *Hail and Farewell,* so I will
stop on the admission that no further attempt was
made to educate me. Between the ages of fifteen
and twenty-one I read most of the English poets,
and when I was twenty-five my love of poetry began
to wilt in *Les Orientales, Les Feuilles d'Automne,
Les Contemplations;* and *La Légende des Siècles*
carried with it the dismal conviction that I had lost
my taste for poetry. Something has broken in me,

[13]

I said; can it be else, for here is beautiful poetry, and I can distinguish in it no more than sonorous versification.

Balzac opened up a new world to me, a world of things, and in Balzac I found a poem so beautiful that I began to think that perhaps my love of poetry was not as dead as I thought it was. . . . But I must not detain the reader from the sonnet:

LA TULIPE

Moi, je suis la tulipe, une fleur de Hollande
Et telle est ma beauté que l'avare Flamand
Paye un de mes oignons plus cher qu'un diamant,
Si mes fonds sont bien purs, si je suis droite et
    grande.

Mon air est féodal, et, comme une Yolande
Dans sa jupe à longs plis étoffée amplement,
Je porte des blasons peints sur mon vêtement
Gueules fascées d'argent, or avec pourpre en bande

Le jardinier divin a filé de ses doigts
Les rayons du soleil et la pourpre des rois
Pour me faire une robe à trame douce et fine.

Nulle fleur du jardin n'égale ma splendeur,
Mais la nature, hélas! n'a pas versé d'odeur
Dans mon calice fait comme un vase de Chine.

Fait comme un vase de Chine is a signature, and in the words *Si je suis droite et grande* the tulip is heard speaking, and again in the words *Mon air est féodal.* And if Balzac had not included two other samples

[14]

of Lucien de Rubempré's poetic genius and Gautier had not spoken, *La Tulipe* might have gone down the centuries as the subject of an everlasting controversy; but the two other samples he printed, one by Madame de Girardin (the authorship of the third has slipped my memory), wear such a pale, keepsake air that suspicion could have hardly failed to gather in the minds of the least wary. All poetry was equally indifferent to Balzac. Gautier, in his great portrait, quotes a line remarkable for three mistakes in French prosody; one mistake, two mistakes, but three mistakes in a single line is a unique achievement. Gautier led me to Mendès (Judith Gautier was the whilom wife of Mendès), and Mendès began my initiation into French poetry by putting Villon into my hands. I was always alive to the beauty of the world and needed but one beautiful sonnet to recover myself, and my own dear self I found in Villon's ballade to his mother. The old woman, I said, will live as long as the French language; her son's verses preserve her better than spices, essences, oils, and the many various swaddles of Egyptian undertakers. And the fair helm-maker will live, and with a life as intense—but why helm-maker? As there is nothing in the poem to show that the old woman got her living by making helmets, and as Villon's poems are usually about lights-of-love, we may assume that the phrase is but a figure of speech. The meaning, however, of the title need not detain us; it is enough for us to know that despite the disapproval expressed over their garden walls

[15]

of Taſte and Fashion the ballade of *La Grosse Margot* will continue to be admired as long as culture exiſts in Europe, and afterwards in some diſtant isle when culture has retired from Europe. Parnassus will always find a home somewhere,

and in this faith I wish to live and die.

Sainte-Beuve remarks pithily that Taſte and Fashion are next door neighbours. He might have added: art's eternal enemies, engaged in eternal warfare with the Muses, victory and defeat going alternately to either side. The Muses receive a crushing defeat; Parnassus is invaded; but the invaders are driven back by the Muses. And then Taſte and Fashion come to terms with the Muses for a brief moment and we wonder if Taſte and Fashion have at laſt learnt something of the nature of art, so pleasingly and so gliby do they discuss Belleau's *April* with Erato and Melpomene:

> Avril, la grace et le ris
> > De Cypris,
> Le flair et la douce haleine;
> Avril, le parfum des dieux,
> > Qui des cieux
> Sentent l'odeur de la plaine;
>
> C'est toy, courtois et gentil,
> > Qui d'exil
> Retire ces passageres,
> Ces arondelles qui vont
> > Et qui sont
> Du printemps les messageres.

And the reason may be stated why we are in these poems at the heart of poetry: because these poems were born of admiration of the only permanent world, the world of things. Ideas, thoughts, reflections, become common quickly; an idea is mine to-day, yours to-morrow, and the day after to-morrow it is on the barrel organs. Every ten years morality, patriotism, duty, and religion, take on meanings different from those they wore before, and that is why each generation, dissatisfied with the literature that preceded it, is inspired to write another literature round the new morality, the new patriotism, the new duty, the new religion, a literature which seems to the writers more permanent than the literature their fathers wrote, but which is destined to pass away as silently. Of the passing of literature there is no end; the world is littered with dead literature as with leaves, and the thought pursues us that the romantic movement which seemed as eternal as the hills thirty years ago is preparing to leave us. Mr. Gosse has climbed into the crow's-nest and thinks he discerns Pope and perhaps Cowper on the horizon. Last week he quoted:

The poplars are fell'd; farewell to the shade,
And the whispering sound of the cool colonnade,

lines that will be admired by men of letters and by whomsoever shall happen upon these lines, for there are always poplars in the world and men will always enjoy the whispering sound of a leafy avenue; but all that is essentially Cowper, his thoughts, his medi-

[17]

tations, his ideas, have passed away, never to return. Wherefore the lines I have quoted do not undermine, rather do they uphold the belief that time cannot wither nor custom stale poetry unsicklied o'er with the pale cast of thought. Again we fall to thinking: Shakespeare never soiled his songs with thought; we commit them to memory almost unconsciously; we remember the objective passages of *The Ancient Mariner,* and no lines of Keats are better known than:

> Deep in the shady sadness of a vale
> Far sunken from the healthy breath of morn,
> Far from the fiery noon, and eve's one star,
> Sat grey-haired Saturn, quiet as a stone,
> Still as the silence round about his lair;
> Forest on forest hung about his head
> Like cloud on cloud.

The poem as it proceeds becomes more reflective, and Keats may have abandoned the subject for that reason, it seeming to him to lack the innocency of a Greek poem, which he desired ardently whilst yielding to pressure from without. The hub of an empire is not favourable to innocency of vision, and it would need a robuster faith than ours to believe that were Shakespeare's songs written by a modern poet they would not be sneered at in the Press as art for art's sake and the poet adjured to tell us instead large, noble and eternal truths about humanity. Tennyson yielded to the large needs of humanity (we know with what result), and many other poets might be named that have been devoured one by one by the needs of the empire. Which shall it be, art or empire? A grave subject for reflection this is, though the choice is not given to us, and if it were, there is little doubt which would get the vote, a fact that will not deter me from writing in this introduction that what modern art lacks is not instruction (of that it has enough and more than enough), but innocency of vision, a gift that our ancestors retained from the cradle to the grave, but which is very soon quenched in these modern times and derided in the newspapers as art for art's sake, a phrase that probably dropped off the pen of some flippant, unthinking journalist, and which attained currency for no better reason than that it supplied the tea-shop and the bus with a convenient catch-word. It has been babbled for the last thirty or forty years, very few caring to ask themselves if art could be produced for other than aesthetic reasons, and the few that did fall to thinking do not seem to have discovered that art for art's sake means pure art, that is to say, a vision almost detached from the personality of the poet. So perhaps the time has come for somebody to ask if there is not more poetry in things than in ideas, and more pleasure in Gautier's *Tulipe* than in Wordsworth's ecclesiastical, political, and admonitory sonnets. My father used to admire the sonnet on Westminster Bridge, and I admired it until I could no longer escape from the suspicion that it was not the beautiful image of a city overhanging a river at dawn that detained the poet, but the hope that he might once more discern a soul in nature. Having, I said to myself, discerned a soul in a primrose by a river's brim, it would seem to him parsimonious to limit the habitation of the soul to a woodland flower, and he would soon begin to seek it in bricks and mortar. But what would he do with the soul when he got it? And after reading the sonnet again and considering the general tone of it, I discovered a carefully concealed morality in it. He would Christianise the soul in nature if he got it, I said; wherefore the poem comes under the heading of proselytism in poetry. If my dear friend, John Eglinton, were here I would press this out and out Wordsworthian to deny that it is Gautier's avoidance of moral questions in his sonnet which lifts *La Tulipe* to a higher plane than Keats's sonnet to Autumn. A fine sonnet is Keats's, no doubt, only blighted here and there with the subjective taint. But we should seek to lead rather than to drive; the goad should be applied only as a last resource, as Stevenson discovered in the Cevennes; Modestine should never be asked to take more than one step at a time without pausing. Such thoughts as these abate proselytising zeal, and to abate my zeal for John's conversion I ask myself, and reproachfully, how many years went by before the seed sown by Gautier *rose from the dreams of its wintry nest.*

But if the thought was long in coming into print, it persisted in me, trying at different moments to lift its head, but always unavailingly till the day when

Impressions and Opinions was cast out of the canon and I began to look round for new subjects. What, said I to myself, about a discussion on pure poetry? And as the title of the new book, *Conversations in Ebury Street,* forbade the essay, I could not do else than invite Mr. John Freeman and Mr. Walter De La Mare to dinner with a view to reporting our conversation, with their consent, of course:

II

MOORE. My dear De La Mare, Wordsworth and grouse cannot be discussed together; each demands our exclusive attention, and the birds to which I am helping you arrived from Scotland last Monday and reached their highest flavour this evening. And the friend who sent them includes in his presents of game presents of vegetables; he likes his asparagus to overlap his peas and his peas to overlap his beans, and so my dinners are often seasonable.

DE LA MARE. Your long residence in France has raised up in you an inveterate hatred of vegetables boiled in water; and you watched us help ourselves to bread sauce with contempt.

MOORE. Bread sauce has always seemed to me more suitable to little birds just taken out of the nest than to men and women; but it may be, as De La Mare says, that I caught the prejudice in France. Boiled chicken has never appeared on this table.

FREEMAN. I was surprised to see turbot.

MOORE. A flabby, tasteless fish, which for thirty

years I ate in full belief of its supremacy, like any other Englishman.

DE LA MARE. And when and how was the discovery made that turbot is a flabby, tasteless fish? Was it your palate that turned against it suddenly, or did some words heard accidentally awaken a latent dislike?

MOORE. Our taste in art purifies with age, and it may be that there is an advancement in our palates which the fishmonger does not take into account, for it is almost impossible in London to get any fish except soles, whiting, cod, haddock, salmon, salmon trout. We may get an occasional brill or plaice, but shad, the finest of all fish, has not been eaten in London for the last fifty years. Shad used to come to London from Holland, but whosoever would eat shad now must go to France in May. Shad comes up the Loire in May, bringing an unimaginable delight to men. Shad and bass are not unlike, but bass comes after shad, a long way before salmon, yet we have to go to France to get this fish. And our grey mullet is sent to France, why I have never been able to find out. The fishmongers tell me that Londoners are too stupid to eat it, but my belief is that the fishmongers have, for reasons which I cannot penetrate, decided that we shall live without bass or mullet. The fault may be with Billingsgate, and the boycott of bass may in the end oblige me to organise a Bass Club. If I could get a hundred members, Billingsgate would have to submit. We will have coffee in the drawing-room, Mabel. And you, Freeman, will you have some more wine? And you, De La Mare? No? Then we may as well go upstairs. You do not smoke cigars, De La Mare? Freeman, I know, doesn't. I was sorry I could not offer you a cigarette the last time you were here, but this evening you will find some in a little sandal-wood box, a tea-caddy of old time, for I dislike the usual silver box—well, as I dislike turbot; the two go together. And I have returned to cigars after a long absence with some misgivings, for every cigar in the box is not worth smoking, no matter what price you pay a hundred. I doubt if the pleasure one gets from a good cigar is a sufficient recompense for the disappointment of a bad one. You will both dine with me on the occasion of the lecture on Shelley and Spenser?

DE LA MARE. I don't know that I shall give the lecture again in London.

MOORE. Then I must read it, for I don't think I can be beguiled out of London even by Shelley and Spenser. What a happy association of names! Together the twin Muses arise before me: Erato and Melpomene.

FREEMAN. A lecture is written to be heard, not read. It will certainly be given again and you must hear it, and should De La Mare fail to inform you of the date, I will.

MOORE. Pray do so, for though I am but a prose writer to-day I read poetry ardently, almost passionately in my youth.

FREEMAN. You said at dinner that you read poetry till you were thirty.

MOORE. And after thirty I hardly looked into a poetry book.

DE LA MARE. Poetry book! You would shock us, but we will not be shocked. How the words——

MOORE. Here is Mabel, come with our coffee.

DE LA MARE. How the words *poetry book* evoke the trim Victorian parlour with all its paraphernalia: rep sofa, wax fruits, and the murmur of the quiet Sunday afternoon coming in through the open window.

FREEMAN. We know that some men come into the world without the poetic sense——

MOORE. I am not sure that you are right, Freeman; indeed, I am sure that you are quite wrong, and that if a search were made among the private papers of lawyers, doctors, and even colonels in the army, we should find a great number of verses, hundreds and thousands, all written before the writers passed from the twenties into the thirties.

FREEMAN. But the verses you would find would be doggerel.

MOORE. Very likely they would be; but opinions vary about verses and I am making for facts: that everybody, or nearly everybody, writes verses between twenty and thirty.

DE LA MARE. Love verses.

MOORE. The larger part of every poetry book consists of verses about love, not of the best poetry but of the best popular poetry, and no doubt a large proportion of the verses we should find if we were to search among the private papers of lawyers,

[24]

doctors, colonels, policemen and Cabinet Ministers, would be no more than love calls. Even so, you would be puzzled to answer why this love poetry should cease at thirty, for the love call doesn't cease then, not till long afterwards.

FREEMAN. Are you sure that doctors and lawyers do not continue to write poetry after thirty?

MOORE. Most men read and write poetry between fifteen and thirty and afterwards very seldom, for in youth we are attracted by ideas, and modern poetry being concerned almost exclusively with ideas we live on duty, liberty and fraternity as chameleons are said to live on light and air, till at last we turn from ideas to things, thinking that we have lost our taste for poetry, unless, perchance, we are classical scholars.

DE LA MARE. I am beginning to understand. You would set a new poetic standard.

MOORE. You give a lofty interpretation to a humble enterprise. If you will bear with me I'll continue a little longer. I submit that it is rare to approach life except through interpretive codes: glosses learnt by heart before any attempt is made to read the text, theories of life so thoroughly assimilated that even the exceptional intelligence after a brief survey is glad to take refuge in authority and tradition. The Dean of St. Paul's is an exemplar of the power of education and circumstance to mute the intelligence, if not to mute the intelligence, to mute at least the expression of the intelligence and to make it the humble servant of conventions and prejudices.

He knows quite well, for instance, that incest as a sin is an invention of the modern world. The Pharaohs nearly always married their sisters; in ancient Persia a son married his mother, and the fruit of the union was considered sacred. The Dean, as I say, knows quite well that horror of incest is one of our modern conventions, but if he were asked he would give it as his opinion that Lord Byron was guilty of a very great sin when he lay with his half-sister; yet we admit marriage between first cousins. Cousins on the father's as well as on the mother's side may marry, and these are more nearly related than a sister is to her half-brother. The Dean of St. Paul's knows, too, that sodomy is essentially a Christian sin. He knows that the Greeks, to whom we owe our civilisation and to whom we are inferior in all the arts, married to continue the race but did not love their wives except in rare instances, yet modern conventions might compel him to advocate or at least to acquiesce in the persecution of those afflicted with abnormal love.

FREEMAN. The moral code has been continually sifted for the last two thousand years.

MOORE. Since the birth of the Christ idea.

FREEMAN. If you like to put it so; and it is not easy to believe that after all these moral siftings we are no nearer to the truth than the Greeks were.

MOORE. Our ideas of beauty have coarsened in the years you speak of.

FREEMAN. But in morals we have a clearer vision.

[26]

MOORE. I see now that I was wrong to introduce morals into my argument or discourse. You would have understood me better if I had refrained, and I will return without more ado to aesthetics and ask if I am not right when I say that no literary critic, however gifted, would have been able to convince the public of sixty years ago that Shelley wasted half of his life writing about liberty. None was born with a finer intelligence than Shelley, and yet the simple inference that to have liberty we must renounce liberty, was not grasped by him; it seemed to lie outside his consciousness. The other day I began to read *Hellas,* but could not continue reading, despite the beauty of the verses, so vague was his apprehension of what he was writing about: liberty. Wordsworth advocated duty as strenuously as Shelley had advocated liberty, and he would have been as unable to put a meaning on the word duty as Shelley would have been to put a meaning on the word liberty. None would deny that Mill's was a first-rate intelligence, yet he was duped like everybody else; he delighted in duty. And the explanation of the discarding of the idea of liberty for the idea of duty becomes plain when we remember that the examination of the Bible, begun in the sixteenth century, began to yield its fruit in eighteen-sixty or seventy. Some will call it Dead Sea fruit, some will call it the immortal fruit of the years, but we are poets and unconcerned with public morality. The fact is enough that in the 'sixties belief in God was

[27]

replaced by belief in morality, and very delighted were the converts to the new creed at their escape from heaven and hell; all the same, they felt cold and ſtrove to keep themselves warm by reading and writing odes to duty. Now, to conclude my little exordium, to which you have liſtened with great patience, I would like to read a few lines from *The Excursion,* lines that were much admired when I was a boy:

> Possessions vanish, and opinions change,
> And passions hold a fluctuating seat:
> But, by the ſtorms of circumſtance unshaken,
> And subject neither to eclipse nor wane,
> Duty exiſts;—immutably survive,
> For our support, the measures and the forms,
> Which an abstract intelligence supplies,
> Whose kingdom is where time and space are not:
> Of other converse, which mind, soul, and heart,
> Do, with united urgency, require,
> What more, that may not perish?   Thou dread
>   Source,
> Prime, self-exiſting Cause and End of all,
> That in the scale of being fill their place,
> Above our human region, or below,
> Set and ſuſtained;

It may be doubted if anybody to-day would claim these lines as poetry—but there again I am bringing into my argument or discourse extraneous matter which had much better be left out, for what I wish to draw your attention to is that an idea which was so near to Wordsworth is so remote from us that we hardly understood what Gilbert meant when he introduced the Slave of Duty into *The Pirates of Penzance*. Morality has gone the way of duty; we call it Victorianism, and when Tennyson's *Idyls* are mentioned everybody smiles. No doubt the ideas of liberty, duty, and morality will return, but the poetry they once inspired will not. Why are you smiling, Freeman? You think that when maidens become chaste we shall again consider Tennyson a great poet?

FREEMAN. My thoughts had wandered to Carlyle's description of Coleridge snuffling: Subjectivity! Objectivity! as he came across a lawn. A wonderful essay this is, but the cruelty of it is near to savagery. We may speak plainly of each other, but it is doubtful if any man has the right to spit upon another and befoul him.

MOORE. As only a eunuch can befoul another. How dare this impotent Scot speak contemptuously of the author of *Christabel!*

> The night is chill; the forest bare;
> Is it the wind that moaneth bleak?
> There is not wind enough in the air
> To move away the ringlet curl
> From the lovely lady's cheek——
> There is not wind enough to twirl
> The one red leaf, the last of its clan,
> That dances as often as dance it can,
> Hanging so light, and hanging so high,
> On the topmost twig that looks up at the sky.

Time cannot wither nor custom stale a dream-flower like this one; creating out of itself, the mind gave birth belike to immortality.

FREEMAN. The lines are magical lines, wonderful as cloud or flower, and they must have come to the poet in a dream, a waking dream, maybe.

MOORE. No lines of such aerial beauty, rainbow beauty, stellar beauty, are in Wordsworth.

DE LA MARE. Coleridge outlived Wordsworth's influence, but there was a time when the poems of Wordsworth and Coleridge were indistinguishable. But Wordsworth is not altogether without objective poetry.

MOORE. There are passages here and there, but no whole poems.

FREEMAN. Do you know *The Green Linnet?*

MOORE. I cannot recall it.

FREEMAN. Then you have not read it; for whosoever has read it, if he have the poetic sense, remembers *The Green Linnet* to the end of his life.

MOORE. I beg of you to repeat it.

FREEMAN. I would not trust my memory. Would you trust yours, De La Mare?

DE LA MARE.

> Beneath these fruit-tree boughs that shed
> Their snow-white blossoms on my head,
> With brightest sunshine round me spread
>   Of spring's unclouded weather,
> In this sequestered nook how sweet
> To sit upon my orchard seat!
> And birds and flowers once more to greet,
>   My last year's friends together.

One have I marked, the happiest guest
In all this covert of the blest:
Hail to Thee, far above the rest
    In joy of voice and pinion!
Thou, Linnet! in thy green array,
Presiding Spirit here to-day,
Dost lead the revels of the May;
    And this is thy dominion.

While birds, and butterflies, and flowers,
Make all one band of paramours,
Thou, ranging up and down the bowers,
    Art sole in thy employment;
A Life, a Presence like the Air,
Scattering thy gladness without care,
Too blest with any one to pair;
    Thyself thy own enjoyment.

Amid yon tuft of hazel trees,
That twinkle to the gusty breeze,
Behold him perched in ecstasies,
    Yet seeming still to hover;
There! where the flutter of his wings
Upon his back and body flings
Shadows and sunny glimmerings,
    That cover him all over.

My dazzled sight he oft deceives,
A Brother of the dancing leaves;
Then flits, and from the cottage eaves
    Pours forth his song in gushes;
As if by that exulting strain
He mocked and treated with disdain
The voiceless Form he chose to feign,
    While fluttering in the bushes.

MOORE. Having found so much pleasure in the bird's plumage and song I think he might have omitted:

The voiceless Form he chose to feign.

FREEMAN. If you can endure no poetry except a description of the external world, your reading will be confined practically to Shakespeare's songs.

MOORE. I shall be glad to re-read these songs, almost forgotten by me. Meanwhile, do you quote one.

FREEMAN. Which do you think, De La Mare?

DE LA MARE. If you have in mind the song in praise of the owl and the cuckoo: *While greasy Joan doth keel the pot,* recite it.

FREEMAN. The song which the curate, the schoolmaster, the clown, and others sing at the end of *Love's Labours Lost.*

SPRING

I

When daisies pied and violets blue
　　And lady-smocks all silver-white
And cuckoo-buds of yellow hue
　　Do paint the meadows with delight,
The cuckoo then, on every tree,
　　Mocks married men; for thus sings he,
　　　　　　Cuckoo;
Cuckoo, cuckoo; O word of fear,
Unpleasing to a married ear!

II

When shepherds pipe on oaten ſtraws,
    And merry larks are ploughmen's clocks,
When turtles tread, and rooks, and daws,
    And maidens bleach their summer smocks,
The cuckoo then, on every tree,
Mocks married men; for thus sings he,
               Cuckoo;
Cuckoo, cuckoo; O word of fear,
Unpleasing to a married ear!

III

When icicles hang by the wall,
    And Dick the shepherd blows his nail,
And Tom bears logs into the hall,
    And milk comes frozen home in pail,
When blood is nipp'd, and ways be foul,
Then nightly sings the ſtaring owl,
               Tu-whit;
Tu-who, a merry note,
While greasy Joan doth keel the pot.

IV

When all aloud the wind doth blow,
    And coughing drowns the parson's saw,
And birds sit brooding in the snow,
    And Marian's nose looks red and raw,
When roaſted crabs hiss in the bowl,
Then nightly sings the ſtaring owl,
               Tu-whit;
Tu-who, a merry note,
While greasy Joan doth keel the pot.

MOORE. My dear friends, I have a proposal to lay before you. If you approve of my definition of pure poetry, something that the poet creates outside of his own personality, we three might compile a book that would be a real advancement in the study of poetry—an anthology of pure poetry, the only one that is lacking on the book-stalls.

FREEMAN. An entertaining idea at the first thought of it. What do you say, De La Mare?

DE LA MARE. Many of the most beautiful poems in the language would have to be barred; for instance, Shelley's lines written in dejection on the seashore near Naples:

The sun is warm, the sky is clear,
    The waves are dancing fast and bright,
Blue isles and snowy mountains wear
    The purple noon's transparent light:
The breath of the moist earth is light
    Around its unexpanded buds;
Like many a voice of one delight,
    The winds, the birds, the ocean floods,
The City's voice itself is soft, like Solitude's.

In the next two stanzas Shelley writes subjectively, but he begins in the third stanza to see himself as a tired child:

Yet now despair itself is mild,
    Even as the winds and waters are;
I could lie down like a tired child,
    And weep away the life of care
Which I have borne and yet must bear,

[34]

Till death like sleep might steal on me,
And I might feel in the warm air
My cheek grow cold, and hear the sea
Breathe o'er my dying brain its last monotony.

MOORE. The value of the anthology, if we compile it, would be that it creates a new standard. Of course, we should have to explain in the introduction why we discarded one poem and kept another.

FREEMAN. And the reasons for omitting a certain poem will be almost as entertaining as the reasons for the retention of another.

DE LA MARE. We shall find as many as a hundred and fifty if we search the Elizabethans thoroughly. Fletcher wrote beautiful lyrics; he will yield many pages. There's Ben Jonson, and——

FREEMAN. Should we not look further back than the Elizabethans? Spenser—but I am afraid he will yield nothing of what we want. There is Skelton.

DE LA MARE. I like Skelton, a true poet, a darling poet; but we must not trust our memories. It is so long since I have read *The Nut-Brown Maid*—and you, Freeman, do you remember it enough to tell us that it contains no hint of subjectivity?

FREEMAN. If we are overstrict I doubt if we shall find a hundred pages of pure poetry.

DE LA MARE. We must draw a strict line, for our anthology rests upon it.

FREEMAN. Moore regrets that Wordsworth could not keep back the words: Voiceless Form.

DE LA MARE. Which may be interpreted that he could not admire the green linnet without intimating that there is a soul in Nature.

FREEMAN. Milton does not abound in objective poetry, Pope still less, but we shall find several poems that come within our definition in the *Songs of Innocence*, none, I am afraid, in the *Songs of Experience*. From Shelley we shall gather a handful: the *Hymn to Pan* and *The Cloud*. Would you admit *The Cloud*, De La Mare?

DE LA MARE. *The Cloud* is not so good a poem as the *Hymn to Pan*, but it comes within our definition.

MOORE. There is *The Sensitive Plant;* a more beautiful description of a garden was never written.

DE LA MARE. But he includes an Indian maiden in the second part, and he ends the poem with a morality:

> It is a modest creed, and yet
> Pleasant if one considers it,
> To own that death itself must be,
> Like all the rest, a mockery.

MOORE. I see your point, but why not the first part of *The Sensitive Plant?*

DE LA MARE. If you admit a right of search for objective stanzas our quest will never end. The most beautiful poetry in *The Ancient Mariner* is the objective poetry——

FREEMAN. And the inclusion of these passages will be a criticism of poetry.

[36]

DE LA MARE.   Yes; but I think we had better limit
the anthology to complete poems.

FREEMAN.   I am afraid we shall find very little in
Keats.

DE LA MARE.   I doubt if we shall find anything.
We can't have the *Ode to a Grecian Urn;* it is barred
by its subjectivity, likewise the *Ode to the Nightin-
gale. The Eve of St. Agnes* is a long narrative
poem——

FREEMAN.   If we are not to have a single quota-
tion from Keats——

DE LA MARE.   There is only one way of settling
our differences, and that is to put the poems to the
vote; any poem that doesn't receive two votes will
be rejected.

MOORE.   Keats never attracted me.   I know he is
the fashion, but I am more interested in my own
than in other people's taste, and I think of him too
frequently as a pussy cat on a sunny lawn.   In Poe—

DE LA MARE.   We shall find many poems in Poe.
There is, of course, the poem *To Helen:*

> Helen, thy beauty is to me
>   Like those Nicéan barks of yore,
> That gently, o'er a perfumed sea,
>   The weary, wayworn wanderer bore
>   To his own native shore.
>
> On desperate seas long wont to roam,
>   Thy hyacinth hair, thy classic face,
> Thy Naiad airs have brought me home
>   To the glory that was Greece,
>   And the grandeur that was Rome.

Lo! in yon brilliant window niche
How statue-like I see thee stand,
The agate lamp within thy hand!
Ah, Psyche, from the regions which
Are Holy Land!

The last lines of *The Raven* exclude the poem from our anthology:

Take thy beak from out my heart, and take thy
form from off my door!
Quoth the raven, Nevermore.

Our difficulty with Poe will be not to overburden our pages with him. We shall have to consider *Dreamland*:

By a route obscure and lonely,
Haunted by ill angels only,
Where an Eidolon, named Night,
On a black throne reigns upright,
I have reached these lands but newly
From an ultimate dim Thule——
From a wild weird clime that lieth, sublime,
Out of Space—out of Time.

And there can be little doubt that we must include *The City in the Sea*:

Lo! Death has reared himself a throne
In a strange city lying alone
Far down within the dim West.

We are all agreed about *The City in the Sea*? And *Eulalie*:

[38]

        I dwelt alone
        In a world of moan,
And my soul was a stagnant tide,
Till the fair and gentle Eulalie became my blushing
        bride——

FREEMAN. No! No! No!
MOORE. No! No! No!
DE LA MARE. Ah, less—less bright
            The stars of the night
            Than the eyes of the radiant girl!

ALL. No! No! No!
DE LA MARE. Eulalie has found no supporters.
What about *The Haunted Palace?*

        In the greenest of our valleys
            By good angels tenanted,
        Once a fair and stately palace—
            Radiant palace—reared its head.

MOORE. Yes.
DE LA MARE. And you, Freeman?
FREEMAN. Yes.
DE LA MARE. *The Haunted Palace* goes in.
Among the late poems *The Bells*——
FREEMAN. A trick! A trick!
DE LA MARE. The beautiful poem *To Helen,* the
second one, contains some subjective lines which I
think you will agree debars it. *Eldorado* is a beau-
tiful poem, but we agreed to accept nothing but
poems of the first rank.   Then there is *Ulalume:*

>The skies they were ashen and sober;
>   The leaves they were crispéd and sere——

MOORE. I am wholeheartedly for *Ulalume*.

FREEMAN. I am not wholeheartedly for *Ulalume*, but I am for its inclusion.

DE LA MARE. We have come down to modern times, and it behooves us to make sure that we have not overlooked anybody of first importance in this preliminary investigation.

MOORE. Landor!

DE LA MARE. An august soul, and yet we overlooked him!

FREEMAN. Landor's prose has obscured the beauty of his verse.

DE LA MARE. I confess my ignorance, I will not say unblushingly but without hesitation, and I doubt, Freeman, if you know Landor much better than I do. But Moore reads little else and will tell us what to seek in Landor.

MOORE. In *Gebir* a shepherd tells another how a nymph came up one night from the sea and engaged with him in a wrestling match, the terms of which were that he should receive *sinuous shells of pearly hue* if he were the victor, and that she should receive from him, if she were the victor, a sheep:

>Now came she forward eager to engage,
>But first her dress, her bosom then survey'd,
>And heav'd it, doubting if she could deceive
>Her bosom seem'd, inclos'd in haze like heav'n,
>To baffle touch, and rose forth undefined:

[40]

Above her knee she drew the robe succinct,
Above her breast, and just below her arms.
This will preserve my breath when tightly bound,
If struggle and equal strength should so constrain.
Thus, pulling hard to fasten it, she spake,
And, rushing at me, closed: I thrill'd throughout
And seem'd to lessen and shrink up with cold.
Again with violent impulse gusht my blood,
And hearing nought external, thus absorb'd,
I heard it, rushing through each turbid vein,
Shake my unsteady swimming sight in air.
Yet with unyielding though uncertain arms
I clung around her neck; the vest beneath
Rustled against our slippery limbs entwined:
Often mine springing with eluded force
Started aside and trembled till replaced:
And when I most succeeded, as I thought,
My bosom and my throat felt so comprest
That life was almost quivering on my lips,
Yet nothing was there painful: these are signs
Of secret arts and not of human might;
What arts I can not tell; I only know
My eyes grew dizzy and my strength decay'd;
I was indeed o'ercome . . . With what regret,
And more, with what confusion, when I reacht
The fold, and yielding up the sheep, she cried,
This pays a shepherd to a conquering maid.
She smiled, and more of pleasure than disdain
Was in her dimpled chin and liberal lip,
And eyes that languisht, lengthening, just like love.
She went away; I on the wicker gate
Leant, and could follow with my eyes alone.
The sheep she carried easy as a cloak;

But when I heard its bleating, as I did,
And saw, she hastening on, its hinder feet
Struggle, and from her snowy shoulder slip,
One shoulder its poor efforts had unveil'd,
Then all my passions mingling fell in tears;
Restless then ran I to the highest ground
To watch her; she was gone; gone down the tide;
And the long moon-beam on the hard wet sand
Lay like a jasper column half up-rear'd.

DE LA MARE.   The lines:

And the long moon-beam on the hard wet sand
Lay like a jasper column half up-rear'd,

are very beautiful.

MOORE.   The incident is complete in itself but we can have *The Hamadryad* if you don't like the poem. It surprises me to find Landor writing *its* bleating, and a little lower down he speaks of *its* hinder feet, as if the sheep were an inanimate object.   And the word *hooves* being available, I am puzzled to find a reason for *hinder feet*.

DE LA MARE.   A poem of several hundred lines will destroy the symmetry of our anthology.   None of the poems we have provisionally accepted exceed a hundred.

MOORE.   A hundred lines, I think, was the length that a poem should never exceed, according to Poe, and the reason he gives is that a poem should be read in one uninterrupted mood of increasing exaltation.   He wrote little and I have never read that he wrote with ease, as Shelley did, but he wrote certainly out of an emotive imagination; his poems are almost free from thought, and that is why we have gathered so many in his tiny garden for our anthology. Another thing. He is one of the few modern poets who wrote with his eyes as well as his ears; Browning saw nothing, Tennyson only a little and with an effort.

FREEMAN. Morris.

DE LA MARE. Poetry is not painting.

MOORE. No; nor is it music. Poetry stands between music and painting, sharing their qualities. We hear the word music applied to poetry, but poetry only touches on music inasmuch as poetry and music both rejoice in rhythm. Music has intervals, and limiting music to the treble clef, to thirteen notes and to a singer's voice, which, if he be a good singer, has a range of two octaves, we get a richness of sound far beyond anything that ten syllables can give. But should the poet open his eyes and tell us all that his eyes see, as Morris did, Melpomene and Erato will not be judged less beautiful than their sisters. In *Golden Wings* our eyes and ears enjoy equally, and so complete is our enjoyment that whilst we read we clap our hands (speaking figuratively) and thank heaven that we have escaped at last from grey thoughtfulness into a world of things:

> Midways of a wallèd garden,
>   In the happy poplar land,
>   Did an ancient castle stand,
> With an old knight for a warden.

Many scarlet bricks there were
    In its walls, and old grey stone;
    Over which red apples shone
At the right time of the year.

On the bricks the green moss grew,
    Yellow lichen on the stone,
    Over which red apples shone;
Little war that castle knew.

Deep green water fill'd the moat,
    Each side had a red-brick lip,
    Green and mossy with the drip
Of dew and rain; there was a boat

Of carven wood, with hangings green
    About the stern; it was great bliss
    For lovers to sit there and kiss
In the hot summer noons, not seen.

The poem takes its name, *Golden Wings,* from the
lyric which Morris introduces into the narrative:

        Gold wings across the sea,
        Moonlight from tree to tree,
        Gold hair beside my knee;
        Ah, sweet knight, come to me,
        Gold wings across the sea.

        Are not my blue eyes sweet?
        The west wind from the wheat
        Blows cold across my feet;
        Is it not time to greet
        Gold wings across the sea?

I will not answer for the accuracy of the quotation.

DE LA MARE. May we include *The Lady of Shalott?*

MOORE. Certainly, the one poem whereby poor Tennyson justifies his existence. The knights as they ride in the morning early through the barley—how does it go, De La Mare, how does it go?

DE LA MARE.

> All in the blue unclouded weather
> Thick-jewell'd shone the saddle-leather,
> The helmet and the helmet feather
> Burn'd like one burning flame together,
>   As he rode down to Camelot.
> As often thro' the purple night,
> Below the starry clusters bright,
> Some bearded meteor, trailing light,
>   Moves over still Shalott.

MOORE. How beautiful! How like Morris!

DE LA MARE. It is not like Morris; it is Morris.

MOORE. And was written probably before Morris. I remember now that the volume entitled *The Defence of Guenevere* was published in 'fifty-seven. *The Lady of Shalott* must have been written in the 'forties. But Tennyson had not the genius to continue the style that he had discovered accidentally, or he was beguiled and yielded himself to moralities and mumbled them till he was eighty.

FREEMAN. *The Lady of Shalott* comes well within our definition, but is it good enough? Is it a better lyric than:

Now sleeps the crimson petal, now the white;
Nor waves the cypress in the palace walk;
Nor winks the gold fin in the porphyry font:
The fire-fly wakens: waken thou with me.

DE LA MARE. Those verses will not get my vote.
A better poem, in my opinion, is *Blow, bugle, blow.*
MOORE. You are forgetting the last verse:

O love, they die in yon rich sky,
    They faint on hill or field or river;
Our echoes roll from soul to soul,
    And grow for ever and for ever.
Blow, bugle, blow, set the wild echoes flying,
And answer, echoes, answer, dying, dying, dying.

The Victorian could never reconcile himself to finishing a poem without speaking about the soul, and the lines are particularly vindictive. I really couldn't stand it, De La Mare:

Our echoes roll from soul to soul,

and worse still:

And grow for ever and for ever.

Are our souls then plants?
DE LA MARE. I had forgotten the soul, and the roll and the roll. Moreover, the first two stanzas are not good enough for us to relax our conditions. I can think of nothing in Swinburne, unless the Spring Chorus from *Atalanta;* it begins well but ends lamely, and in one line he writes:

[46]

And the hooféd heel of a satyr crushes
    The chestnut-husk at the chestnut-root.

A chestnut has no husk; the outer shell is the shuck.
And in the next stanza we read:

    And Pan by noon and Bacchus by night,
    Fleeter of foot than the fleet-foot kid.

You, Moore, do not like the word *feet* applied to
hoofed animals, but I think we might concede some-
thing, for though Pan has hooves Bacchus has not.

MOORE. I do not see why he shouldn't have said
the fleet-hooved kid, but I dare say I am pedantic.
Husk, as you say, is not as correct as *shuck,* but these
are not reasons for omitting the poem, and my vote
is given to it.

DE LA MARE. And mine.

FREEMAN. And mine.

DE LA MARE. And now, Freeman, we must be
thinking of our train to Anerley.

MOORE. A drink of some sort before you start on
this wild journey?

DE LA MARE. Nothing for me.

FREEMAN. Nor for me. We have worked well
this evening, and laid down a foundation——

MOORE. Of poetry and of morality.

FREEMAN. Of morality! Our aim has been to
leave it out.

MOORE. However slyly we build, morality always
finds an unguarded loophole, and to stir up their lan-
guid emotions the younger poets and poetesses are

[47]

obliged to engage themselves in marriage. I have heard that they often stoop, for the sake of a poem, to irregular relations; but we'll not go into that. After playing at love for about a month or more the poem begins to curdle in their brains, and when that falls out the moment for parting has come. I see them in my thoughts going forth into the country; stopping at the cross-roads they speak: My way is to the left, thine is to the right; we have hoped and sorrowed together, and in future time . . . and so on. I think you know the rest of that poem, both of you.

DE LA MARE. There is a good deal of that poetry going about. Do you think we shall put an end to it by raising the standard?

FREEMAN. Forgive me for interrupting you, De La Mare, but I would ask Moore if he has a title in mind for our anthology.

MOORE. A title? Of course! *Pure Poetry.*

III

And keeping the words pure poetry in mind I returned to the drawing-room to consider if a sifting of our literature would bring to light a hundred and fifty pages of pure poetry; and my thoughts turning on Milton I remembered how Beelzebub used to drive me to *Prometheus Bound.* A rich, gnarled style, I continued, can be discovered in Milton, but he could not reconcile the Jew and the Greek. And I wasted much time on an imaginary essay in which

[48]

I sought to prove that the cosmopolitan Jew of the Carlton Hotel and the White Star line is no nearer to art than the Palestinian tribesman. At the sound of a train whistle coming over the garage at the back of my house my thoughts returned from Moab, whither they had wandered, and I remembered the young poets that I had described as trooping into the country in pairs, in search of subjects for free verse: My way is to the left, yours is to the right. We have hoped and sorrowed together, and in future time. . . .

For lack of imagination these poets and poetesses pour their quaking moralities and their sighing amorousness into the ears of Calliope and Thalia, who turn away abashed and ask: Where are your bodies? The poets and poetesses cry: We are ashamed of our bodies, but we are proud of our souls. The two Muses of grave mien answer: You would do well to consult Erato. And the pretty Muse crowned with roses appears to the poets and poetesses, saying: You suffer from cold? With a shiver they answer the Muse, who tells them that she needs the body even more than the soul, and it amused me to think for a little while of the pretty Muse crowned with roses talking like this; and a moment after I began to think that I was on the trail of a choice subject, one that would have suited my dear friend Clutton-Brock, who would have disentangled it as well as another, unless indeed it might be still better disentangled in the form of a satiric drama in which the poets and poetesses would debate whether free verse would enable those who had nothing to say to write smoothly. The Muses would answer: Free verse, like free steam, is powerless, but confine steam, and confine verse within the limits of a ten-syllable line with rich rhymes, and a great power is generated. The poets and poetesses cry: Steam was unknown in Parnassus. Muses talking about machinery and cog-wheels—fie upon you! Thalia and Melpomene answer: Although we abide no longer on the Grecian hill, we are not unmindful of the present world. After strophe and antistrophe comes the epode, and I began to foresee a delightful epode, the poets and poetesses confessing to the Muses that they write trilogy after trilogy without troubling to invent anything: All we need for a trilogy is a young woman who visits us. And the poetesses cry: All we need for our trilogies is a young man who kisses us. Muses, hear us. Surely in every human life there is enough subject matter for a trilogy, wherefore every human being can produce a trilogy, not only one trilogy but many trilogies. Every ten years of life can be turned into a trilogy. A poet is among us who has dragged out of twenty-four hours more pages than there are in a hundred Greek dramas; I have fallen short of the mark—a thousand Greek dramas. The only break, said I to myself, in this desolating tide of subjectivity is *Riceyman Steps,* the most objective of all novels, more than any that I have written myself. The temptation came stealing by to allow my midnight thoughts to harden into a critical essay, but fortunately my eyes happened at that moment to alight on some pictures on the walls, and I said: Objectivity in its relation to literature has been considered sufficiently, and on Saturday night in Vale Avenue I will introduce objectivity in painting to the company. My word! what interesting things might be said on that subject; and whilst waiting for the dawn I asked myself if Velasquez were not the most objective of all painters.

He seems to have looked on king, queen, and infanta with a cold, melancholy detachment, which some critics have attributed to the court of Philip IV, and they may be pardoned for doing so, so difficult is it for us to estimate the effect of etiquette on the soul in a court in which the etiquette was so strict that it was a capital offence, punishable by death, for a man to stretch forth his hand to save the queen from falling. But circumstance cannot deepen or lighten the colour of a man's mind; if we bring anything into the world it is the colour of our minds, and what is the colour of our minds but fate? and what is fate but character? In thinking of Velasquez we translate the tone of silvery-grey that pervades all his canvases into a moral quality: melancholy, concluding that his melancholy—he need not have been aware of it—was his gift, which, despite his almost excessive realism, allowed him to remain an aesthetic painter.

But Hals, though as objective a painter as Velasquez, was not susceptible to melancholy nor even regret. His mind was a giggling, ale-house mind,

[51]

and as painting presented no difficulty to him he painted with unwearying touch jerkins, ruffs, sword hilts, blond beards, curled moustaches, jewelled gauntlets, doffed and donned as the occasion required, seeking, so it seems, always a showy aspect for his sitters. Those who had fine profiles turned them to the audience, like actors; those who fancied their eyes are painted in full face; those who preferred dignity to admiration are in three-quarter face. A gross joviality prevails in every face, but even junketting is not safe against *ennui;* pleasure's deadly enemy was there, no doubt, but Hals's gusto blinded him to it, and we may be sure that no thought of the wives asleep peaceably under quilts and canopies disturbed his mind, wives soon to be awakened for their mates' pleasure, gross livers truly even as their husbands, and it may be argued that gross men must have gross wives, and we ask ourselves whether the gross wife produces the gross husband, or the gross husband the gross wife, and unable to find an answer to this perplexing question we forget morals in our admiration of Hals's touch, a touch that never fails in the representation of all that the greedy eye sees. For the painter to fix his eye on the object and to work forgetful of all else except the object and his representation of it, is half the battle, but half the battle does not mean victory. If it did a photograph would be a picture, and an accurate report of a conversation fine literature. But art needs something more than mere verisimilitude; call it, reader, what name you please, but agree

[52]

with me in this : that the essential cannot be acquired or faked. All comes under this law, yet Hals, whose mind was all ale-house, lived down the ale-house completely, and I know no pleasanter legend than that this big, jovial Dutchman lay in prison for nearly twenty years, acquiring on bread and water the soul that was denied to him in health and abundance. At eighty he reappears in Haarlem painting a group of old women paupers in an alms-house, and the picture shows that whilst retaining all his craft, he had gained something that he did not possess in his youth. Fromentin did not like these pictures—these pictures, I say, for the group of old women was followed by a group of old men which remained unfinished, death having snatched palette and brushes from Hals's hands. Fromentin, who was a poet of a sort, a painter of a sort and a beautiful prose writer, liked the strutting burgomasters better, and in *Les Maîtres d'autrefois*—which I cannot quote from, the volume having disappeared from my shelves, he laments that the generation of painters and critics that succeeded him admire the loose handling in these two last pictures, mere sensations of tone and colour they were to him, for a painter never wanders far from his own palette; wherever he finds it he worships, and Fromentin discovering a sublimated Fromentin in Franz Hals, fell down on his knees and prayed.

Courbet, who preceded Manet by a few years, ranks high among modern painters, but there is very little pleasure in his painting, and whosoever pos-

sesses his pictures (and a great many do) must be
hard set to choose a room in which to hang them,
for they are not in keeping with a drawing-room,
and they are not in keeping with a study. It would
be hard to say what carpet should be laid down or
how a room should be furnished in which there are
Courbets. Despite his great capacity as a painter
his pictures do not interest us in public galleries;
very often they repel us. We like them best in
picture-dealers' shops, perhaps because nothing is
permanent there, and if you would press me still
further, I would say that a picture by Courbet would
be more in keeping in a peasant's cottage than else-
where. But there is no wall space in a peasant's
cottage. If, however, I may say, without seeming
frivolous, that pictures recall perfumes, I would say
that Courbet's pictures recall the smell of a smoky
cottage more than any other pictures that I can think
of at this moment. My comparison is not frivolous;
many pictures do recall perfumes. Boucher's cer-
tainly recall the perfume of bathwater and fine linen,
and Manet's recall the springtime; they are as fra-
grant. Manet's world is as young as Botticelli's,
and sitting opposite to me at dinner Monet has often
broken the silence with the words: How like Manet
is to his painting! Manet once said to me: Vollon's
fish are worthless, for they are not like fish; mine
are. And he would accept no reason for putting his
fish above Vollon's except the reason he gave him-
self: that they were more like fish. It seemed like
a slight to his art to admit that his paintings were

[54]

more beautiful than Courbet's because his mind was a finer mind, and he listened, pleased but supercilious, when I said: Your lovely greys and your pinks are part of your mind, and Courbet's bottle-green forests are part of his mind. He was aware, of course, that Courbet's green was *vert de bouteille,* but I do not think he apprehended very clearly that Courbet's desire to shock every year in the Salon was a peasant's instinct. He would have liked to do so himself, but his finer instincts held him forbidden. . . . I can tell an anecdote that will bring Courbet and Manet before the reader. Once on a time there was a painter called Français who painted landscapes spick and span as well-kept gardens, and on being asked what he thought of one of these in the Salon, Courbet answered: In every landscape there is a place to crap, and in Français's I can never find the spot. Manet, when he went to see Meissonier's *Battle of Friedland,* said: Magnificent! Everything in it is iron except the breastplates. And in these criticisms we have the aesthetic confessions of two great painters, Courbet a peasant of genius, Manet a witty, light-hearted, Parisian gentleman, typically French, less complete than Hals, more witty and agreeable, less lofty and disdainful than Velasquez, and not less profound. So we would like to think, or perhaps we do think, in a way, despite a haunting suspicion that this appreciation will awaken fierce resentment.

The reader will notice that neither Poussin's, Rembrandt's, nor Ingres's name has been mentioned,

[55]

and it would be pleasant indeed to follow the play and interplay of objectivity and subjectivity in these examples; but it seems to me that the theme can be developed better through other examples, through Corot and Claude. The pictures Corot painted in Rome were beautifully-drawn domes, roofs, and arcades, with a sullen river beneath, and in our National Gallery there is the dome of St. Peter's seen in the distance through overarching boughs. An arid subject this would seem to be, and one very unlikely to find a customer, and no doubt many years had to pass before it found one. But in the beginning of his life, when art was upon him, Corot did not think about customers, and feeling that he could draw as well as Claude, he continued to seek subjects on his return from Rome that a painter of less natural genius would turn from. An erstwhile friend of mine is the possessor of a picture of a factory yard in which there is neither tree nor plant nor flower, only yellow sand and yellow sandstone walls and high-pitched, blue-slated roofs. In the middle distance is another building with a high-pitched roof, blue slates and an iron gateway, and the only relief from this desert ugliness is a shadow thrown across the foreground by a building outside of the picture. We have seen Parisian workmen sawing through great blocks of sandstone, and we have met the blocks on lorries drawn by six great grey Normandy horses in charge of a carter, who cracks a loud whip and calls upon them, but not on the great docile beast in the shafts; he knows his

business so well that he needs no telling, and the saw-
yers and the carters of the yellow sandstone will
help the reader to see the factory that Corot saw
under an almost cloudless June sky. When he un-
dertook to find a picture in this very unpictorial sub-
ject, he looked forward to interrupting the monot-
ony of the foreground with a beautiful brown
shadow, and his thoughts passing on to the long,
narrow windows, he began to think how by beautiful
drawing they might be made to seem more beautiful
than they really were; and how the iron railings
could also be redeemed by good drawing, and the
tone of the high-pitched roof varied, for the slates
were only violet in certain hours of the day. Above
the roof was the blue air, and he knew he could get
its depths and contrast its airy lightness with the
grimness below. The picture was now in his head
and seeing warm tones of yellow and brown every-
where, he composed his palette, his thoughts return-
ing to Rome. A subtle aesthetician it would be who
could determine whether this picture was an early
or a middle-period picture painted in his early style.
In the life of every artist there are sudden advance-
ments and sudden returnings. But why waste time
in conjectures when a visit to the library can give us
a fact? Because conjectures are often more inter-
esting than facts and more improving to the mind.
The encyclopaedia cannot tell us everything, happily,
and no date has any biographer put upon Corot's
discovery of the sentimental willow. A picture-
dealer may have shown him a newspaper in which

the critic said that Corot could not paint the French country, only Italy, and a challenge is always inspiring; or it may have been that Corot was asked by some friends who lived in the country to spend Sunday with them, friends who lived by a river shadowed by poplars (which is most sentimental, a poplar or a willow?). Corot, who had never observed the French country before, returned at once to Ville d'Avray, and brought back poplars and willows that were sold for large sums of money. Nor is it impossible that he wished to die a rich man, and having once caught sight of a fisherman putting forth, he could never resist again the temptation of a boat with a fisher in it, his snood showing through the greenery like a red anemone, a fisher who never caught a fish but drew a great draft of dollars out of a city situated by a lake in the Middle West.

And whilst thinking how I had met him in the woods of Ville d'Avray my thoughts began to droop and would have passed into nothingness if the church clock striking two had not roused me. We cannot be far off now from the dawn, about an hour, mayhap two, for the month is August. The travellers are in their beds with their wives, sleeping. And thinking it would be better to be asleep than sitting in filmy light thinking unpleasant things of Corot I struggled upstairs, between sleeping and waking recalling the words we had exchanged—with difficulty, for my brain was fuddled with sleep: A beautiful picture, master, is beginning on your canvas, but I can't find your foreground in nature. My fore-

[58]

ground is two hundred yards ahead, he answered. That was in 'seventy-four or 'seventy-five, in the last years of his life, when he found willows everywhere, principally in his own head. Subjectivity, objectivity . . . Tristan or the Mastersingers: which will last the longer? Which will be admired fifty years hence? . . . to bed, to bed!

TO MISTRESS ISABEL PENNELL

BY Saint Mary, my lady,
Your mammy and daddy
Brought forth a goodly baby,
  My maiden Isabel,
Reflaring rosabel,
The fragrant camamel,
  The ruddy rosary,
The sovereign rosemary,
The pretty strawberry,
  The columbine, the nepte,
The ieloffer well set,
The proper violet
  Envied your colour
Is like the daisy flower
After the April shower,
  Star of the morrow grey,
The blossom on the spray,
The freshest flower of May,
  Maidenly demure,
Of womanhood the lure.
Wherefore I make you sure
  It were an heavenly health,
It were an endless wealth,
A life for God himself
  To hear this nightingale
Among the birdes small
Warbling in the vale—
    Dug, dug,
    Jug, jug,
Good year and good luck,
With chuk, chuk, chuk, chuk.

                          John Skelton

SPRING, the sweet Spring, is the year's pleasant king;
Then blooms each thing, then maids dance in a ring.
Cold doth not sting, the pretty birds do sing,
Cuckoo, jug, jug, pu we, to witta woo.

The palm and may make country houses gay,
Lambs frisk and play, the shepherds pipe all day,
And we hear aye birds tune this merry lay,
Cuckoo, jug, jug, pu we, to witta woo.

The fields breathe sweet, the daisies kiss our feet,
Young lovers meet, old wives a-sunning sit,
In every street these tunes our ears do greet,
Cuckoo, jug, jug, pu we, to witta woo.
      Spring, the sweet Spring!
Thomas Nashe

THE PASSIONATE SHEPHERD TO HIS LOVE

COME live with me and be my Love,
And we will all the pleasures prove
That hills and valleys, dale and field,
And all the craggy mountains yield.

There will we sit upon the rocks
And see the shepherds feed their flocks,
By shallow rivers, to whose falls
Melodious birds sing madrigals.

There will I make thee beds of roses
And a thousand fragrant posies,
A cap of flowers, and a kirtle
Embroider'd all with leaves of myrtle.

A gown made of the finest wool,
Which from our pretty lambs we pull,
Fair linéd slippers for the cold,
With buckles of the purest gold.

A belt of straw and ivy buds
With coral clasps and amber studs:
And if these pleasures may thee move,
Come live with me and be my Love.

Thy silver dishes for thy meat
As precious as the gods do eat,
Shall on an ivory table be
Prepared each day for thee and me.

The shepherd swains shall dance and sing
For thy delight each May morning:
If these delights thy mind may move,
Then live with me and be my Love.

Christopher Marlowe

[63]

LAWN as white as driven snow,
Cyprus black as e'er was crow;
Gloves as sweet as damask roses;
Masks for faces and for noses;
Bugle bracelet, necklace amber,
Perfume for a lady's chamber;
Golden quoifs and ſtomachers,
For my lads to give their dears:
Pins and poking-ſticks of ſteel,
What maids lack from head to heel:
Come buy of me, come; come buy, come buy;
Buy, lads, or else your lasses cry:
Come buy.

William Shakeſpeare

THE poor soul sat sighing by a sycamore tree,
  Sing all a green willow;
Her hand on her bosom, her head on her knee,
  Sing willow, willow, willow:
The fresh streams ran by her, and murmur'd her
    moans;
  Sing willow, willow, willow;
Her salt tears fell from her, and soften'd the stones;
  Sing willow, willow, willow;
  Sing all a green willow must be my garland.
Let nobody blame him; his scorn I approve,—
I call'd my love false love; but what said he then?
  Sing willow, willow, willow:
If I court moe women, you'll couch with moe men.

William Shakespeare

WHERE the bee sucks, there suck I:
In a cowslip's bell I lie;
There I couch when owls do cry.
On the bat's back I do fly
After summer merrily.
Merrily, merrily shall I live now
Under the blossom that hangs on the bough.

William Shakespeare

NOW the hungry lion roars,
    And the wolf behowls the moon;
Whilst the heavy ploughman snores,
    All with weary task fordone.
Now the wasted brands do glow,
    Whilst the screech-owl, screeching loud,
Puts the wretch that lies in woe
    In remembrance of a shroud.
Now it is the time of night
    That the graves all gaping wide,
Every one lets forth his sprite,
    In the church-way paths to glide:
And we fairies, that do run
    By the triple Hecate's team,
From the presence of the sun,
    Following darkness like a dream,
Now are frolic: not a mouse
Shall disturb this hallow'd house:
I am sent with broom before,
To sweep the dust behind the door.

Enter OBERON *and* TITANIA *with their train.*

OBE. Through the house give glimmering light,
    By the dead and drowsy fire:
Every elf and fairy sprite
    Hop as light as bird from brier;
And this ditty, after me,
Sing, and dance it trippingly.
TITA. First, rehearse your song by rote,
    To each word a warbling note:

Hand in hand, with fairy grace,
Will we sing, and bless this place.
                    [*song and dance.*
OBE. Now, until the break of day,
    Through this house each fairy stray.
    To the beſt bride-bed will we,
    Which by us shall blessed be;
    And the issue there create
    Ever shall be fortunate.
    So shall all the couples three
    Ever true in loving be;
    And the blots of Nature's hand
    Shall not in their issue ſtand;
    Never mole, hare lip, nor scar,
    Nor mark prodigious, such as are
    Despised in nativity,
    Shall upon their children be.
    With this field-dew consecrate,
    Every fairy take his gait:
    And each several chamber bless,
    Through this palace, with sweet peace;
    And the owner of it bleſt
    Ever shall in safety reſt.
    Trip away; make no ſtay;
    Meet me all by break of day.
                    William Shakeſpeare

COME unto these yellow sands,
And then take hands:
Courtsied when you have and kiss'd
The wild waves whist,
Foot it featly here and there;
And, sweet sprites, the burthen bear.
Hark, hark!
Bow-wow.
The watch-dogs bark:
Bow-wow.
Hark, hark! I hear
The strain of strutting chanticleer
Cry, Cock-a-diddle-dow.

William Shakespeare

FULL fathom five thy father lies;
Of his bones are coral made;
Those are pearls that were his eyes:

Nothing of him that doth fade
But doth suffer a sea-change
Into something rich and strange.
Sea-nymphs hourly ring his knell:
                              Ding-dong.
Hark! now I hear them,—Ding-dong, bell
William Shakespeare

WHEN daisies pied and violets blue
   And lady-smocks all silver-white
And cuckoo-buds of yellow hue
   Do paint the meadows with delight,
The cuckoo then, on every tree,
Mocks married men; for thus sings he,
                Cuckoo;
Cuckoo, cuckoo: O word of fear,
Unpleasing to a married ear!

When shepherds pipe on oaten straws
   And merry larks are ploughmen's clocks,
When turtles tread, and rooks, and daws,
   And maidens bleach their summer smocks,
The cuckoo then, on every tree,
Mocks married men; for thus sings he,
                Cuckoo;
Cuckoo, cuckoo: O word of fear,
Unpleasing to a married ear!

When icicles hang by the wall
   And Dick the shepherd blows his nail
And Tom bears logs into the hall
   And milk comes frozen home in pail,
When blood is nipp'd and ways be foul,
Then nightly sings the staring owl,
                Tu-whit;
Tu-who, a merry note,
While greasy Joan doth keel the pot.

When all aloud the wind doth blow
   And coughing drowns the parson's saw

And birds sit brooding in the snow
  And Marian's nose looks red and raw,
When roasted crabs hiss in the bowl,
Then nightly sings the staring owl,
                    Tu-whit;
Tu-who, a merry note,
While greasy Joan doth keel the pot.
                    William Shakespeare

WHO IS SILVIA?

WHO is Silvia? what is she,
   That all our swains commend her?
Holy, fair and wise is she;
   The heaven such grace did lend her,
That she might admired be.

Is she kind as she is fair?
   For beauty lives with kindness.
Love doth to her eyes repair,
   To help him of his blindness,
And, being help'd, inhabits there.

Then to Silvia let us sing,
   That Silvia is excelling;
She excels each mortal thing
   Upon the dull earth dwelling:
To her let us garlands bring.
            William Shakespeare

YOU spotted snakes with double tongue,
 Thorny hedgehogs, be not seen;
Newts and blind-worms, do no wrong,
 Come not near our fairy queen.

 Philomel, with melody
 Sing in our sweet lullaby;
Lulla, lulla, lullaby, lulla, lulla, lullaby:
 Never harm,
 Nor spell nor charm,
 Come our lovely lady nigh;
 So, good night, with lullaby.

Weaving spiders, come not here;
 Hence, you long-legg'd spinners, hence!
Beetles black, approach not near;
 Worm nor snail, do no offence.

 Philomel, with melody,
 Sing in our sweet lullaby;
Lulla, lulla, lullaby, lulla, lulla, lullaby:
 Never harm,
 Nor spell nor charm,
 Come our lovely lady nigh;
 So, good night, with lullaby.

William Shakespeare

OVER hill, over dale,
   Thorough bush, thorough brier,
Over park, over pale,
   Thorough flood, thorough fire,
I do wander every where,
Swifter than the moon's sphere;
And I serve the fairy queen,
To dew her orbs upon the green.
The cowslips tall her pensioners be:
In their gold coats spots you see;
Those be rubies, fairy favours,
In those freckles live their savours:
I must go seek some dewdrops here
And hang a pearl in every cowslip's ear.

William Shakespeare

UNDER the greenwood tree
Who loves to lie with me,
And turn his merry note
Unto the sweet bird's throat;
Come hither, come hither, come hither:
Here shall he see
No enemy
But winter and rough weather.

Who doth ambition shun
And loves to live i' the sun,
Seeking the food he eats
And pleased with what he gets,
Come hither, come hither, come hither:
Here shall he see
No enemy
But winter and rough weather.

JAQ. I'll give you a verse to this note that I made
yesterday in despite of my invention.
AMI. And I'll sing it.
JAQ. Thus it goes:—

If it do come to pass
That any man turn ass,
Leaving his wealth and ease,
A stubborn will to please,
Ducdame, ducdame, ducdame:
Here shall he see
Gross fools as he,
An if he will come to me.

William Shakespeare

[76]

O MISTRESS mine, where are you roaming?
O, stay and hear; your true love's coming,
    That can sing both high and low:
Trip no further, pretty sweeting;
Journeys end in lovers meeting,
    Every wise man's son doth know.

What is love? 'tis not hereafter;
Present mirth hath present laughter;
    What's to come is still unsure:
In delay there lies no plenty;
Then come kiss me, sweet and twenty,
    Youth's a stuff will not endure.
                    William Shakespeare

COME away, come away, death,
  And in sad cypress let me be laid;
Fly away, fly away, breath;
  I am slain by a fair cruel maid.
My shroud of white, stuck all with yew,
    O, prepare it!
My part of death, no one so true
    Did share it.

Not a flower, not a flower sweet,
  On my black coffin let there be strown;
Not a friend, not a friend greet
  My poor corpse, where my bones shall be thrown:
A thousand thousand sighs to save,
    Lay me, O, where
Sad true lover never find my grave,
    To weep there!

William Shakespeare

WHEN that I was and a little tiny boy,
  With hey, ho, the wind and the rain,
A foolish thing was but a toy,
  For the rain it raineth every day.

But when I came to man's estate,
  With hey, ho, the wind and the rain,
'Gainst knaves and thieves men shut their gate,
  For the rain it raineth every day.

But when I came, alas! to wive,
  With hey, ho, the wind and the rain,
By swaggering could I never thrive,
  For the rain it raineth every day.

But when I came unto my beds,
  With hey, ho, the wind and the rain,
With toss-pots still had drunken heads,
  For the rain it raineth every day.

A great while ago the world begun,
  With hey, ho, the wind and the rain,
But that's all one, our play is done,
  And we'll strive to please you every day.

William Shakespeare

WHAT SHALL HE HAVE THAT KILL'D THE DEER?

WHAT shall he have that kill'd the deer?
His leather skin and horns to wear.
    Then sing him home;
Take thou no scorn to wear the horn;
It was a crest ere thou wast born:
    Thy father's father wore it,
    And thy father bore it:
The horn, the horn, the lusty horn
Is not a thing to laugh to scorn.

William Shakespeare

WHEN daffodils begin to peer,
  With heigh! the doxy over the dale,
Why, then comes in the sweet o' the year;
  For the red blood reigns in the winter's pale.

The white sheet bleaching on the hedge,
  With heigh! the sweet birds, O, how they sing!
Doth set my pugging tooth on edge;
  For a quart of ale is a dish for a king.

The lark, that tirra-lyra chants,
  With heigh! with heigh! the thrush and the jay,
Are summer songs for me and my aunts,
  While we lie tumbling in the hay.

But shall I go mourn for that, my dear?
  The pale moon shines by night:
And when I wander here and there,
  I then do most go right.

If tinkers may have leave to live,
  And bear the sow-skin budget,
Then my account I well may give,
  And in the stocks avouch it.
                    William Shakespeare

ORPHEUS with his lute made trees,
And the mountain tops that freeze,
   Bow themselves when he did sing:
To his music plants and flowers
Ever sprung; as sun and showers
   There had made a lasting spring.

Every thing that heard him play,
Even the billows of the sea,
   Hung their heads, and then lay by.
In sweet music is such art,
Killing care and grief of heart
   Fall asleep, or hearing, die.

William Shakespeare

HARK, hark! the lark at heaven's gate sings,
　And Phœbus 'gins arise,
His steeds to water at those springs
　On chaliced flowers that lies;
And winking Mary-buds begin
　To ope their golden eyes:
With every thing that pretty is,
　My lady sweet, arise:
　　Arise, arise.

William Shakespeare

NOW winter nights enlarge
 The number of their hours;
And clouds their storms discharge
 Upon the airy towers.
Let now the chimneys blaze
 And cups o'erflow with wine,
Let well-tun'd words amaze
 With harmony divine.
Now yellow waxen lights
 Shall wait on honey love
While youthful revels, masks, and courtly
  sights,
 Sleep's leaden spells remove.

This time doth well dispense
 With lovers' long discourse;
Much speech hath some defence,
 Though beauty no remorse.
All do not all things well;
 Some measures comely tread,
Some knotted riddles tell;
 Some poems smoothly read.
The summer hath his joys,
 And winter his delights;
Though love and all his pleasures are but
  toys,
 They shorten tedious nights.

        Thomas Campion

HAYMAKERS, rakers, reapers and mowers,
    Wait on your Summer-Queen!
Dress up with musk-rose her eglantine bowers,
    Daffodils strew the green!
        Sing, dance and play,
        'Tis holiday!
    The sun does bravely shine
    On our ears of corn.
        Rich as a pearl
        Comes every girl.
This is mine, this is mine, this is mine.
Let us die ere away they be borne.

Bow to our Sun, to our Queen, and that fair one
    Come to behold our sports;
Each bonny lass here is counted a rare one,
    As those in princes' courts.
        These and we
        With country glee,
    Will teach the woods to resound,
    And the hills with echoes hollow.
        Skipping lambs
        Their bleating dams
'Mongst kids shall trip it round;
For joy thus our wenches we follow.

Wind, jolly huntsmen, your neat bugles shrilly,
    Hounds make a lusty cry;
Spring up, you falconers, partridges freely,
    Then let your brave hawks fly!
        Horses amain,
        Over ridge, over plain,

The dogs have the stag in chase:
'Tis a sport to content a king.
So ho! ho! through the skies
How the proud bird flies,
And sousing, kills with a grace!
Now the deer falls; hark! how they ring.

Thomas Dekker

QUEEN and huntress, chaste and fair,
  Now the sun is laid to sleep;
Seated in thy silver chair
  State in wonted manner keep:
    Hesperus entreats thy light,
    Goddess excellently bright.

Earth, let not thy envious shade
  Dare itself to interpose;
Cynthia's shining orb was made
  Heaven to clear when day did close;
    Bless us then with wished sight,
    Goddess excellently bright.

Lay thy bow of pearl apart,
  And thy crystal shining quiver
Give unto the flying hart
  Space to breathe, how short soever,
    Thou that mak'st a day of night,
    Goddess excellently bright.

Ben Jonson

THE owl is abroad, the bat, and the toad,
And so is the cat-a-mountain;
The ant and the mole sit both in a hole,
And the frog peeps out o' the fountain.
The dogs they do bay, and the timbrels play,
The spindle is now a-turning;
The moon it is red, and the stars are fled,
But all the sky is a-burning:
The ditch is made, and our nails the spade,
With pictures full, of wax and of wool;
Their livers I stick with needles quick;
There lacks but the blood to make up the flood.
Quickly, dame, then, bring your part in!
Spur, spur, upon little Martin,
Merrily, merrily, make him sail,
A worm in his mouth and a thorn in his tail,
Fire above, and fire below,
With a whip in your hand, to make him go!

Ben Jonson

CUPID AND MY CAMPASPE PLAY'D

CUPID and my Campaspe play'd
At cards for kisses; Cupid paid:
He stakes his quiver, bow, and arrows,
His mother's doves, and team of sparrows;
Loses them too; then down he throws
The coral of his lip, the rose
Growing on's cheek (but none knows how);
With these, the crystal of his brow,
And then the dimple on his chin;
All these did my Campaspe win:
And last he set her both his eyes—
She won, and Cupid blind did rise.
O Love! has she done this to thee?
What shall, alas! become of me?

John Lyly

PACK, clouds, away, and welcome day,
  With night we banish sorrow;
Sweet air blow soft, mount larks aloft
  To give my Love good-morrow!
Wings from the wind to please her mind
  Notes from the lark I'll borrow;
Bird, prune thy wing, nightingale sing,
  To give my Love good-morrow;
    To give my Love good-morrow
    Notes from them both I'll borrow.

Wake from thy nest, Robin-red-breast,
  Sing, birds, in every furrow;
And from each hill, let music shrill
  Give my fair Love good-morrow!
Blackbird and thrush in every bush,
  Stare, linnet, and cock-sparrow!
You pretty elves, amongst yourselves
  Sing my fair Love good-morrow;
    To give my Love good-morrow
    Sing, birds, in every furrow.

                    Thomas Heywood

CALL for the robin-redbreast and the wren,
Since o'er shady groves they hover,
And with leaves and flowers do cover
The friendless bodies of unburied men.
Call unto his funeral dole
The ant, the field mouse, and the mole,
To rear him hillocks that shall keep him warm,
And (when gay tombs are robbed) sustain no harm;
But keep the wolf far thence, that's foe to men,
For with his nails he'll dig them up again.

John Webster

ROSES, their sharp spines being gone,
Not royal in their smells alone,
   But in their hue;
Maiden pinks, of odour faint,
Daisies smell-less, yet most quaint,
   And sweet thyme true;

Primrose, first-born child of Ver,
Merry springtime's harbinger.
   With harebells dim;
Oxlips in their cradles growing,
Marigolds on deathbeds blowing,
   Larks'-heels trim.

All dear Nature's children sweet,
Lie 'fore bride and bridegroom's feet,
   Blessing their sense!
Not an angel of the air,
Bird melodious, or bud fair,
   Be absent hence!

The crow, the slanderous cuckoo, nor
The boding raven, nor chough hoar,
   Nor chattering pie,
May on our bride house perch or swing,
Or with them any discord bring
   But from it fly!

               John Fletcher

SWEET Echo, sweetest nymph, that liv'st unseen
   Within thy airy shell,
  By slow Meander's margent green,
And in the violet-embroidered vale,
  Where the love-lorn nightingale
Nightly to thee her sad song mourneth well;
Canst thou not tell me of a gentle pair
   That likest thy Narcissus are?
     O, if thou have
   Hid them in some flowery cave,
    Tell me but where,
Sweet queen of parly, daughter of the sphere?
So mayst thou be translated to the skies,
And give resounding grace to all heaven's harmonies.
John Milton

NOW the bright morning-star, day's harbinger,
Comes dancing from the east, and leads with her
The flowery May, who from her green lap throws
The yellow cowslip and the pale primrose.
Hail, bounteous May! that dost inspire
Mirth, and youth, and warm desire;
Woods and groves are of thy dressing,
Hill and dale doth boast thy blessing.
Thus we salute thee with our early song,
And welcome thee, and wish thee long.

John Milton

THE wanton troopers riding by
Have shot my fawn, and it will die.
Ungentle men! they cannot thrive
To kill thee. Thou ne'er didst alive
Them any harm; alas! nor could
Thy death yet do them any good.
I'm sure I never wished them ill;
Nor do I for all this, nor will:
But, if my simple prayers may yet
Prevail with Heaven to forget
Thy murder, I will join my tears
Rather than fail. But, O my fears!
It cannot die so. Heaven's king
Keeps register of everything,
And nothing may we use in vain;
Even beasts must be with justice slain,
Else men are made their deodands.
Though they should wash their guilty hands
In this warm life-blood which doth part
From thine, and wound me to the heart,
Yet could they not be clean: their stain
Is dyed in such a purple grain.
There is not such another in
The world, to offer for their sin.
    Unconstant Sylvio, when yet
I had not found him counterfeit,
One morning (I remember well),
Tied in this silver chain and bell,
Gave it to me: nay, and I know
What he said then, I'm sure I do.
Said he, 'Look how your huntsman here

Hath taught a Fawn to hunt his Dear.'
But Sylvio soon had me beguiled:
This waxed tame, while he grew wild,
And quite regardless of my smart,
Left me his Fawn, but took his Heart.

 Thenceforth I set myself to play
My solitary time away
With this, and very well content
Could so mine idle life have spent.
For it was full of sport, and light
Of foot and heart, and did invite
Me to its game: it seemed to bless
Itself in me. How could I less
Than love it? Oh, I cannot be
Unkind to a beaſt that loveth me.

 Had it lived long, I do not know
Whether it too might have done so
As SYLVIO did; his gifts might be
Perhaps as false, or more, than he.
But I am sure, for aught that I
Could in so short a time espy,
Thy love was far more better then
The love of false and cruel men.

With sweeteſt milk and sugar firſt
I it at my own fingers nursed;
And as it grew, so every day
It wax'd more white and sweet than they—
It had so sweet a breath! and oft
I blush'd to see its foot more soft
And white,—shall I say,—than my hand?
Nay, any lady's of the land!

It is a wondrous thing how fleet
'Twas on those little silver feet:

With what a pretty skipping grace
It oft would challenge me the race:——
And when 't had left me far away
'Twould stay, and run again, and stay:
For it was nimbler much than hinds,
And trod as if on the four winds.

I have a garden of my own,
But so with roses overgrown
And lilies, that you would it guess
To be a little wilderness:
And all the spring-time of the year
It only lovèd to be there.
Among the beds of lilies I
Have sought it oft, where it should lie;
Yet could not, till itself would rise,
Find it, although before mine eyes:——
For in the flaxen lilies' shade
It like a bank of lilies laid.

Upon the roses it would feed,
Until its lips e'en seemed to bleed:
And then to me 'twould boldly trip,
And print those roses on my lip.
But all its chief delight was still
On roses thus itself to fill,
And its pure virgin limbs to fold
In whitest sheets of lilies cold:——
Had it lived long, it would have been
Lilies without—roses within.

Oh help! Oh help! I see it faint
And die as calmly as a saint.
See how it weeps! the tears do come

Sad, slowly dropping like a gum.
So weeps the wounded balsam; so
The holy frankincense doth flow;
The brotherless Heliades
Melt in such amber tears as these.
   I in a golden vial will
Keep these two crystal tears, and fill
It till it do o'erflow with mine,
Then place it in DIANA'S shrine.
   Now my sweet fawn is vanished to·
Whither the swans and turtles go;
In fair Elizium to endure,
With milk-like lambs and ermines pure.
Oh do not run too fast: for I
Will but bespeak thy grave, and die.
   First my unhappy statue shall
Be cut in marble; and withal,
Let it be weeping too: but there
The engraver sure his art may spare;
For I so truly thee bemoan,
That I shall weep, though I be stone:
Until my tears, still dropping, wear
My breast, themselves engraving there.
There at my feet shalt thou be laid,
Of purest alabaster made:
For I would have thine image be
White as I can, though not as thee.

Andrew Marvell

TO gather Flowers Sappha went,
  And homeward she did bring
Within her Lawnie Continent
  The treasure of the Spring.

She smiling blusht, and blushing smil'd
  And sweetly blushing thus,
She lookt as she'd been got with child
  By young Favonius.

Her Apron gave (as she did passe)
  An Odor more divine,
More pleasing too, than ever was
  The lap of Proserpine.
                    Robert Herrick

YE have been fresh and green,
    Ye have been fill'd with flowers;
And ye the walks have been
    Where maids have spent their hours.

You have beheld how they
    With wicker arks did come,
To kiss and bear away
    The richer cowslips home.

You've heard them sweetly sing,
    And seen them in a round;
Each virgin, like a spring,
    With honeysuckles crown'd.

But now, we see none here,
    Whose silvery feet did tread,
And with dishevelled hair
    Adorn'd the smoother mead.

Like unthrifts, having spent
    Your stock and needy grown,
You're left here to lament
    Your poor estates alone.

                              Robert Herrick

TO CHARLOTTE PULTENEY

TIMELY blossom, infant fair,
Fondling of a happy pair,
Every morn and every night
Their solicitous delight,
Sleeping, waking, still at ease,
Pleasing, without skill to please;
Little gossip, blithe and hale,
Tattling many a broken tale,
Singing many a tuneless song,
Lavish of a heedless tongue;
Simple maiden, void of art,
Babbling out the very heart,
Yet abandon'd to thy will,
Yet imagining no ill,
Yet too innocent to blush;
Like the linnet in the bush
To the mother-linnet's note
Moduling her slender throat;
Chirping forth thy petty joys,
Wanton in the change of toys,
Like the linnet green, in May
Flitting to each bloomy spray
Wearied then and glad of rest,
Like the linnet in the nest:—
This thy present happy lot
This, in time will be forgot:
Other pleasures, other cares,
Ever-busy Time prepares;
And thou shalt in thy daughter see,
This picture, once, resembled thee.
                    Ambrose Philips

PIPING down the valleys wild
Piping songs of pleasant glee,
On a cloud I saw a child,
And he laughing said to me:

Pipe a song about a Lamb!'
So I piped with merry cheer.
'Piper, pipe that song again';
So I piped: he wept to hear.

'Drop thy pipe, thy happy pipe;
Sing thy songs of happy cheer':
So I sang the same again,
While he wept with joy to hear.

'Piper, sit thee down and write
In a book, that all may read.'
So he vanish'd from my sight,
And I plucked a hollow reed,

And I made a rural pen,
And I stain'd the water clear,
And I wrote my happy songs
Every child may joy to hear.

William Blake

SONG

ʜᴏᴡ sweet I roam'd from field to field
   And taſted all the summer's pride,
Till I the Prince of Love beheld,
   Who in the sunny beams did glide!

He show'd me lilies for my hair,
   And blushing roses for my brow;
He led me through his gardens fair
   Where all his golden pleasures grow.

With sweet May dews my wings were wet,
   And Phœbus fired my vocal rage;
He caught me in his silken net,
   And shut me in his golden cage.

He loves to sit and hear me sing,
   Then, laughing, sports and plays with me;
Then ſtretches out my golden wing,
   And mocks my loss of liberty.
                 William Blake

'I HAVE no name:
I am but two days old.'
What shall I call thee?
'I happy am,
Joy is my name,'
Sweet joy befall thee!

Pretty Joy!
Sweet Joy, but two days old.
Sweet Joy I call thee:
Thou dost smile,
I sing the while,
Sweet joy befall thee!
William Blake

WHEN the green woods laugh with the voice of joy,
And the dimpling stream runs laughing by;
When the air does laugh with our merry wit,
And the green hill laughs with the noise of it;

When the meadows laugh with lively green,
And the grasshopper laughs in the merry scene;
When Mary and Susan and Emily
With their sweet round mouths sing, 'Ha, ha, he!'

When the painted birds laugh in the shade,
Where our table with cherries and nuts is spread,
Come live, and be merry, and join with me,
To sing the sweet chorus of 'Ha, ha, he!'

William Blake

WHEN the voices of children are heard on the green,
And laughing is heard on the hill,
My heart is at rest within my breast,
And everything else is still.

'Then come home, my children, the sun is gone down,
And the dews of night arise;
Come, come, leave off play, and let us away
Till the morning appears in the skies.'

'No, no, let us play, for it is yet day,
And we cannot go to sleep;
Besides, in the sky the little birds fly,
And the hills are all cover'd with sheep.'

'Well, well, go and play till the light fades away,
And then go home to bed.'
The little ones leapèd, and shouted, and laugh'd,
And all the hills echoèd.

William Blake

THE SHEPHERD

HOW sweet is the Shepherd's sweet lot!
From the morn to the evening he strays;
He shall follow his sheep all the day,
And his tongue shall be filled with praise.

For he hears the lamb's innocent call,
And he hears the ewe's tender reply;
He is watchful while they are in peace,
For they know when their Shepherd is nigh.

William Blake

WHEN my mother died I was very young,
And my father sold me while yet my tongue
Could scarcely cry, ' 'Weep! 'weep! 'weep! 'weep!'
So your chimneys I sweep, and in soot I sleep.

There's little Tom Dacre, who cried when his head,
That curl'd like a lamb's back, was shav'd: so I said,
'Hush, Tom! never mind it, for, when your head's
      bare
You know that the soot cannot spoil your white
      hair.'

And so he was quiet, and that very night,
As Tom was a-sleeping, he had such a sight!—
That thousands of sweepers, Dick, Joe, Ned, and
      Jack,
Were all of them lock'd up in coffins of black.

And by came an Angel, who had a bright key,
And he open'd the coffins and set them all free;
Then down a green plain leaping, laughing, they run,
And wash in a river, and shine in the sun.

Then naked and white, all their bags left behind,
They rise upon clouds and sport in the wind;
And the Angel told Tom, if he'd be a good boy,
He'd have God for his father, and never want joy.

And so Tom awoke; and we rose in the dark,
And got with our bags and our brushes to work.
Tho' the morning was cold, Tom was happy and
      warm;
So if all do their duty, they need not fear harm.

William Blake

THE Sun does arise,
And make happy the skies;
The merry bells ring
To welcome the Spring;
The skylark and thrush,
The birds of the bush,
Sing louder around
To the bells' cheerful sound,
While our sports shall be seen
On the Echoing Green.

Old John, with white hair,
Does laugh away care,
Sitting under the oak,
Among the old folk.
They laugh at our play,
And soon they all say:
'Such, such were the joys
When we all, girls and boys,
In our youth-time were seen
On the Echoing Green.'

Till the little ones, weary,
No more can be merry;
The sun does descend,
And our sports have an end.
Round the laps of their mothers
Many sisters and brothers,
Like birds in their nest,
Are ready for rest,
And sport no more seen
On the darkening Green.

William Blake

SPRING

SOUND the flute!
Now it's mute.
Birds delight,
Day and night;
Nightingale
In the dale,
Lark in sky,
Merrily,
Merrily, merrily, to welcome in the year.

Little boy
Full of joy;
Little girl,
Sweet and small;
Cock does crow,
So do you;
Merry voice,
Infant noise,
Merrily, merrily, to welcome in the year.

Little lamb,
Here I am;
Come and lick
My white neck;
Let me pull
Your soft wool;
Let me kiss
Your soft face:
Merrily, merrily, we welcome in the year.

William Blake

OLD Meg she was a gipsy;
   And lived upon the moors,
Her bed it was the brown heath turf,
   And her house was out of doors.
Her apples were swart blackberries,
   Her currants, pods o' broom;
Her wine was dew of the wild white rose,
   Her book a churchyard tomb.

Her brothers were the craggy hills,
   Her sisters larchen trees;
Alone with her great family
   She lived as she did please.
No breakfast had she many a morn,
   No dinner many a noon,
And, 'stead of supper, she would stare
   Full hard against the moon.

But every morn, of woodbine fresh
   She made her garlanding,
And, every night, the dark glen yew
   She wove, and she would sing.
And with her fingers, old and brown,
   She plaited mats of rushes,
And gave them to the cottagers
   She met among the bushes.

Old Meg was as brave as Margaret Queen,
   And tall as Amazon;
An old red blanket cloak she wore,
   A chip-hat had she on:
God rest her aged bones somewhere!
   She died full long agone!

John Keats

KUBLA KHAN

IN Xanadu did Kubla Khan
A stately pleasure-dome decree:
Where Alph, the sacred river, ran
Through caverns measureless to man
Down to a sunless sea.
So twice five miles of fertile ground
With walls and towers were girdled round:
And there were gardens bright with sinuous rills
Where blossom'd many an incense-bearing tree;
And here were forests ancient as the hills,
Enfolding sunny spots of greenery.

But oh! that deep romantic chasm which slanted
Down the green hill athwart a cedarn cover!
A savage place! as holy and enchanted
As e'er beneath a waning moon was haunted
By woman wailing for her demon-lover!
And from this chasm, with ceaseless turmoil seething,
As if this earth in fast thick pants were breathing,
A mighty fountain momently was forced:
Amid whose swift half-intermitted burst
Huge fragments vaulted like rebounding hail,
Or chaffy grain beneath the thresher's flail;
And mid these dancing rocks at once and ever
It flung up momently the sacred river.
Five miles meandering with a mazy motion
Through wood and dale the sacred river ran,
Then reach'd the caverns measureless to man,
And sank in tumult to a lifeless ocean:
And 'mid this tumult Kubla heard from far
Ancestral voices prophesying war!

The shadow of the dome of pleasure
Floated midway on the waves;
Where was heard the mingled measure
From the fountain and the caves.
It was a miracle of rare device,
A sunny pleasure-dome with caves of ice!

A damsel with a dulcimer
In a vision once I saw:
It was an Abyssinian maid,
And on her dulcimer she play'd,
Singing of Mount Abora.
Could I revive within me
Her symphony and song,
To such a deep delight 'twould win me
That with music loud and long,
I would build that dome in air,
That sunny dome! those caves of ice!
And all who heard should see them there,
And all should cry, Beware! Beware!
His flashing eyes, his floating hair!
Weave a circle round him thrice,
And close your eyes with holy dread,
For he on honey-dew hath fed,
And drunk the milk of Paradise.

Samuel Taylor Coleridge

UP, up! ye dames, and lasses gay!
To the meadows trip away.
'Tis you must tend the flocks this morn,
And scare the small birds from the corn.
   Not a soul at home may stay:
     For the shepherds must go
     With lance and bow
   To hunt the wolf in the woods to-day.

Leave the hearth and leave the house
To the cricket and the mouse:
Find grannam out a sunny seat,
With babe and lambkin at her feet.
   Not a soul at home may stay;
     For the shepherds must go
     With lance and bow
   To hunt the wolf in the woods to-day.
              Samuel Taylor Coleridge

HEAR, sweet Spirit, hear the spell,
Lest a blacker charm compel!
So shall the midnight breezes swell
With thy deep long lingering knell.

And at evening evermore,
In a chapel on the shore,
Shall the chaunter, sad and saintly,
Yellow tapers burning faintly,
Doleful masses chaunt for thee,
  Miserere Domine!

Hush! the cadence dies away
  On the quiet moonlight sea:
The boatmen rest their oars and say
  Miserere Domine!
Samuel Taylor Coleridge

SONG

A WIDOW bird sat mourning for her love
    Upon a wintry bough;
The frozen wind crept on above,
    The freezing stream below.

There was no leaf upon the forest bare
    No flower upon the ground,
And little motion in the air
    Except the mill-wheel's sound.
        Percy Bysshe Shelley

AND like a dying lady, lean and pale,
Who totters forth, wrapp'd in a gauzy veil,
Out of her chamber, led by the insane
And feeble wanderings of her fading brain,
The moon arose up in the murky East,
A white and shapeless mass—
                    Percy Bysshe Shelley

THE CLOUD

I BRING fresh showers for the thirsting flowers,
    From the seas and the streams;
I bear light shade for the leaves when laid
    In their noonday dreams.
From my wings are shaken the dews that waken
    The sweet buds every one,
When rocked to rest on their mother's breast,
    As she dances about the sun.
I wield the flail of the lashing hail,
    And whiten the green plains under,
And then again I dissolve it in rain,
    And laugh as I pass in thunder.

I sift the snow on the mountains below,
    And their great pines groan aghast;
And all the night 'tis my pillow white,
    While I sleep in the arms of the blast.
Sublime on the towers of my skyey bowers,
    Lightning my pilot sits;
In a cavern under is fettered the thunder,
    It struggles and howls at fits;
Over earth and ocean, with gentle motion,
    This pilot is guiding me,
Lured by the love of the genii that move
    In the depths of the purple sea;
Over the rills, and the crags, and the hills,
    Over the lakes and the plains,
Wherever he dream, under mountain or stream,
    The Spirit he loves remains;
And I all the while bask in Heaven's blue smile,
    Whilst he is dissolving in rains.

The sanguine Sunrise, with his meteor eyes,
  And his burning plumes outspread,
Leaps on the back of my sailing rack,
  When the morning ſtar shines dead;
As on the jag of a mountain crag,
  Which an earthquake rocks and swings,
An eagle alit one moment may sit
  In the light of its golden wings.
And when Sunset may breathe, from the lit sea be-
    neath,
  Its ardours of reſt and of love,
And the crimson pall of eve may fall
  From the depth of Heaven above,
With wings folded I reſt, on mine aëry neſt,
  As ſtill as a brooding dove.

That orbèd maiden with white fire laden,
  Whom mortals call the Moon,
Glides glimmering o'er my fleece-like floor,
  By the midnight breezes ſtrewn;
And wherever the beat of her unseen feet,
  Which only the angels hear,
May have broken the woof of my tent's thin roof.
  The ſtars peep behind her and peer;
And I laugh to see them whirl and flee,
  Like a swarm of golden bees,
When I widen the rent in my wind-built tent,
  Till the calm rivers, lakes, and seas,
Like ſtrips of the sky fallen through me on high,
  Are each paved with the moon and these.

I bind the Sun's throne with a burning zone,
  And the Moon's with a girdle of pearl;

The volcanoes are dim, and the stars reel and swim,
　　When the whirlwinds my banner unfurl.
From cape to cape, with a bridge-like shape,
　　Over a torrent sea,
Sunbeam-proof, I hang like a roof,—
　　The mountains its columns be.
The triumphal arch through which I march
　　With hurricane, fire, and snow,
When the Powers of the air are chained to my chair,
　　Is the million-coloured bow;
The sphere-fire above its soft colours wove,
　　While the moist Earth was laughing below.

I am the daughter of Earth and Water,
　　And the nursling of the Sky;
I pass through the pores of the ocean and shores;
　　I change, but I cannot die.
For after the rain when with never a stain
　　The pavilion of Heaven is bare,
And the winds and sunbeams with their convex
　　　gleams
　　Build up the blue dome of air,
I silently laugh at my own cenotaph,
　　And out of the caverns of rain,
Like a child from the womb, like a ghost from the
　　　tomb,
　　I arise and unbuild it again.
　　　　　　　　　　　　Percy Bysshe Shelley

ARETHUSA

I

ARETHUSA arose
From her couch of snows
In the Acroceraunian mountains,—
From cloud and from crag,
With many a jag,
Shepherding her bright fountains.
She leapt down the rocks,
With her rainbow locks
Streaming among the streams;—
Her steps paved with green
The downward ravine
Which slopes to the western gleams;
And gliding and springing
She went, ever singing,
In murmurs as soft as sleep;
The Earth seemed to love her,
And Heaven smiled above her,
As she lingered towards the deep.

II

Then Alpheus bold,
On his glacier cold,
With his trident the mountains strook;
And opened a chasm
In the rocks—with the spasm
All Erymanthus shook.
And the black south wind
It unsealed behind
The urns of the silent snow,
And earthquake and thunder
Did rend in sunder
The bars of the springs below.

And the beard and the hair
Of the River-god were
Seen through the torrent's sweep,
As he followed the light
Of the fleet nymph's flight
To the brink of the Dorian deep.

III

'Oh, save me! Oh, guide me!
And bid the deep hide me,
For he grasps me now by the hair!'
The loud Ocean heard,
To its blue depth ſtirred,
And divided at her prayer;
And under the water
The Earth's white daughter
Fled like a sunny beam;
Behind her descended
Her billows, unblended
With the brackish Dorian ſtream:—
Like a gloomy ſtain
On the emerald main
Alpheus rushed behind,—
As an eagle pursuing
A dove to its ruin
Down the ſtreams of the cloudy wind.

IV

Under the bowers
Where the Ocean Powers
Sit on their pearlèd thrones;
Through the coral woods
Of the weltering floods,
Over heaps of unvalued ſtones;

Through the dim beams
Which amid the streams
Weave a network of coloured light;
And under the caves,
Where the shadowy waves
Are as green as the forest's night:—
Outspeeding the shark,
And the sword-fish dark,
Under the Ocean's foam,
And up through the rifts
Of the mountain clifts
They passed to their Dorian home.

v

And now from their fountains
In Enna's mountains,
Down one vale where the morning basks,
Like friends once parted
Grown single-hearted,
They ply their watery tasks.
At sunrise they leap
From their cradles steep
In the cave of the shelving hill;
At noontide they flow
Through the woods below
And the meadows of asphodel;
And at night they sleep
In the rocking deep
Beneath the Ortygian shore;—
Like spirits that lie
In the azure sky
When they love but live no more.

Percy Bysshe Shelley

[123]

WHILE GATHERING FLOWERS ON THE PLAIN OF ENNA

I

SACRED Goddess, Mother Earth,
  Thou from whose immortal bosom
Gods, and men, and beasts have birth,
  Leaf and blade, and bud and blossom,
Breathe thine influence most divine
On thine own child, Proserpine.

II

If with mists of evening dew
  Thou dost nourish these young flowers
Till they grow, in scent and hue,
  Fairest children of the Hours,
Breathe thine influence most divine
On thine own child, Proserpine.

Percy Bysshe Shelley

I

FROM the forests and highlands
  We come, we come;
From the river-girt islands,
  Where loud waves are dumb
    Listening to my sweet pipings.
The wind in the reeds and the rushes
  The bees on the bells of thyme,
The birds on the myrtle bushes,
  The cicale above in the lime,
And the lizards below in the grass,
Were as silent as ever old Tmolus was,
    Listening to my sweet pipings.

II

Liquid Peneus was flowing,
  And all dark Tempe lay
In Pelion's shadow, outgrowing
  The light of the dying day,
    Speeded by my sweet pipings.
The Sileni, and Sylvans, and Fauns,
  And the Nymphs of the woods and the waves,
To the edge of the moist river-lawns,
  And the brink of the dewy caves,
And all that did then attend and follow,
Were silent with love, as you now, Apollo,
    With envy of my sweet pipings.

III

I sang of the dancing stars,
  I sang of the daedal Earth,

And of Heaven—and the giant wars,
And Love, and Death, and Birth,—
And then I changed my pipings,—
Singing how down the vale of Maenalus
I pursued a maiden and clasped a reed.
Gods and men, we are all deluded thus!
It breaks in our bosom and then we bleed:
All wept, as I think both ye now would,
If envy or age had not frozen your blood,
At the sorrow of my sweet pipings.

Percy Bysshe Shelley

EVENING

PONTE A MARE, PISA

THE sun is set; the swallows are asleep;
   The bats are flitting fast in the grey air;
The slow soft toads out of damp corners creep,
   And evening's breath, wandering here and there
Over the quivering surface of the stream,
Wakes not one ripple from its silent dream.

There is no dew on the dry grass to-night,
   Nor damp within the shadow of the trees;
The wind is intermitting, dry, and light;
   And in the inconstant motion of the breeze
The dust and straws are driven up and down
And whirled about the pavement of the town.

Within the surface of the fleeting river
   The wrinkled image of the city lay,
Immovably unquiet, and for ever
   It trembles, but it never fades away;
Go to the [.   .   .   .   ]
You, being changed, will find it then as now.

The chasm in which the sun has sunk is shut
   By darkest barriers of enormous cloud,
Like mountain over mountain huddled—but
   Growing and moving upward in a crowd,
And over it a space of watery blue,
Which the keen evening star is shining through.
                    Percy Bysshe Shelley

AUTUMN

A DIRGE

THE warm sun is failing, the bleak wind is wailing,
The bare boughs are sighing, the pale flowers are
   dying,
              And the year
On the earth her deathbed, in a shroud of leaves
   dead,
              Is lying.
         Come, months, come away,
         From November to May
         In your saddest array;
         Follow the bier
         Of the dead cold year,
And like dim shadows watch by her sepulchre.

The chill rain is falling, the nipt worm is crawling,
The rivers are swelling, the thunder is knelling
              For the year;
The blithe swallows are flown, and the lizards each
   gone
              To his dwelling;
         Come, months, come away,
         Put on white, black, and grey,
         Let your light sisters play—
         Ye, follow the bier
         Of the dead cold year,
And make her grave green with tear on tear.
                          Percy Bysshe Shelley

IN the cowslip pips I lie,
Hidden from the buzzing fly,
While green grass beneath me lies,
Pearled with dew like fishes' eyes,
Here I lie, a clock-a-clay,
Waiting for the time of day.

While the forest quakes surprise,
And the wild wind sobs and sighs,
My home rocks as like to fall,
On its pillar green and tall;
When the pattering rain drives by
Clock-a-clay keeps warm and dry.

Day by day, and night by night,
All the week I hide from sight;
In the cowslip pips I lie,
In rain and dew still warm and dry;
Day and night, and night and day,
Red, black-spotted clock-a-clay.

My home shakes in wind and showers,
Pale green pillar topped with flowers,
Bending at the wild wind's breath,
Till I touch the grass beneath;
Here I live, lone clock-a-clay,
Watching for the time of day.

John Clare

WITHIN a thick and spreading hawthorn bush
   That overhung a molehill, large and round,
I heard from morn to morn a merry thrush
   Sing hymns of rapture, while I drank the sound
With joy—and oft an unintruding guest,
   I watched her secret toils from day to day;
How true she warped the moss to form her nest,
   And modelled it within with wood and clay,
And by and by, like heath-bells gilt with dew,
   There lay her shining eggs as bright as flowers,
Ink-spotted over, shells of green and blue;
   And there I witnessed, in the summer hours,
A brood of nature's minstrels chirp and fly,
Glad as the sunshine and the laughing sky.

John Clare

MARIANA

"MARIANA IN THE MOATED GRANGE"
(Measure for Measure.)

WITH blackest moss the flower-plots
   Were thickly crusted one and all.
The rusted nails fell from the knots
   That held the pear to the gable-wall.
The broken sheds look'd sad and strange:
   Unlifted was the clinking latch;
   Weeded and worn the ancient thatch
Upon the lonely moated grange.
     She only said, 'My life is dreary,
       He cometh not,' she said;
     She said, 'I am aweary, aweary,
       I would that I were dead!'

Her tears fell with the dews at even;
   Her tears fell ere the dews were dried;
She could not look on the sweet heaven,
   Either at morn or eventide,
After the flitting of the bats,
   When thickest dark did trance the sky,
   She drew her casement-curtain by,
And glanced athwart the glooming flats.
     She only said, 'The night is dreary,
       He cometh not,' she said;
     She said, 'I am aweary, aweary,
       I would that I were dead!'

Upon the middle of the night,
   Waking she heard the night-fowl crow:
The cock sung out an hour ere light:
   From the dark fen the oxen's low

Came to her: without hope of change,
  In sleep she seem'd to walk forlorn,
  Till cold winds woke the gray-eyed morn
About the lonely moated grange.
    She only said, 'The day is dreary,
      He cometh not,' she said;
    She said, 'I am aweary, aweary,
      I would that I were dead!'

About a stone-cast from the wall
  A sluice with blacken'd waters slept,
And o'er it many, round and small,
  The cluster'd marish-mosses crept.
Hard by a poplar shook alway,
  All silver-green with gnarled bark:
For leagues no other tree did mark
The level waste, the rounding gray.
    She only said, 'My life is dreary,
      He cometh not,' she said;
    She said, 'I am aweary, aweary,
      I would that I were dead!'

And ever when the moon was low,
  And the shrill winds were up and away,
In the white curtain, to and fro,
  She saw the gusty shadow sway.
But when the moon was very low,
  And wild winds bound within their cell,
The shadow of the poplar fell
Upon her bed, across her brow.
    She only said, 'The night is dreary,
      He cometh not,' she said;
    She said, 'I am aweary, aweary,
      I would that I were dead!'

All day within the dreamy house,
    The doors upon their hinges creak'd;
The blue fly sung in the pane; the mouse
    Behind the mouldering wainscot shriek'd,
Or from the crevice peer'd about.
    Old faces glimmer'd thro' the doors,
    Old footsteps trod the upper floors,
Old voices called her from without.
        She only said, 'My life is dreary,
            He cometh not,' she said;
        She said, 'I am aweary, aweary,
            I would that I were dead!'

The sparrow's chirrup on the roof,
    The slow clock ticking, and the sound
Which to the wooing wind aloof
    The poplar made, did all confound
Her sense; but most she loathed the hour
    When the thick-moted sunbeam lay
    Athwart the chambers, and the day
Was sloping toward his western bower.
        Then, said she, 'I am very weary,
            He will not come,' she said;
        She wept, 'I am aweary, aweary,
            Oh God, that I were dead!'
                                Alfred Tennyson

RHAICOS was born amid the hills wherefrom
Gnidos the light of Caria is discern'd,
And small are the white-crested that play near,
And smaller onward are the purple waves.
Thence festal choirs were visible, all crown'd
With rose and myrtle if they were inborn;
If from Pandion sprang they, on the coast
Where stern Athenè raised her citadel,
Then olive was intwined with violets
Cluster'd in bosses, regular and large.
For various men wore various coronals;
But one was their devotion: 'twas to her
Whose laws all follow, her whose smile withdraws
The sword from Ares, thunderbolt from Zeus,
And whom in his chill caves the mutable
Of mind, Poseidon, the sea-king, reveres,
And whom his brother, stubborn Dis, hath pray'd
To turn in pity the averted cheek
Of her he bore away, with promises,
Nay, with loud oath before dread Styx itself,
To give her daily more and sweeter flowers
Than he made drop from her on Enna's dell.
    Rhaicos was looking from his father's door
At the long trains that hastened to the town
From all the valleys, like bright rivulets
Gurgling with gladness, wave outrunning wave,
And thought it hard he might not also go
And offer up one prayer, and press one hand,
He knew not whose. The father call'd him in,
And said, 'Son Rhaicos! those are idle games;
Long enough I have lived to find them so.'
And ere he ended, sighed, as old men do

Always, to think how idle such games are.
'I have not yet,' thought Rhaicos in his heart,
And wanted proof.

           'Suppose thou go and help
Echeion at the hill, to bark yon oak
And lop its branches off, before we delve
About the trunk and ply the root with axe:
This we may do in winter.'

           Rhaicos went;
For thence he could see farther, and see more
Of those who hurried to the city-gate.
Echeion he found there, with naked arm
Swart-hair'd, strong-sinew'd, and his eyes intent
Upon the place where first the axe should fall:
He held it upright. 'There are bees about,
Or wasps, or hornets,' said the cautious eld,
'Look sharp, O son of Thallinos!' The youth
Inclined his ear, afar and warily,
And cavern'd in his hand. He heard a buzz
At first, and then the sound grew soft and clear,
And then divided into what seem'd tune,
And there were words upon it, plaintive words.
He turn'd, and said, 'Echeion! do not strike
That tree: it must be hollow; for some God
Speaks from within. Come thyself near.' Again
Both turn'd toward it: and behold! there sat
Upon the moss below, with her two palms
Pressing it on each side, a maid in form.
Downcast were her long eyelashes, and pale
Her cheek, but never mountain-ash display'd
Berries of colour like her lips so pure,
Nor were the anemones about her hair
Soft, smooth, and wavering, like the face beneath.
'What dost thou here?' Echeion, half-afraid,

Half-angry, cried.   She lifted up her eyes,
But nothing spake she.   Rhaicos drew one ſtep
Backward, for fear came likewise over him,
But not such fear: he panted, gaspt, drew in
His breath, and would have turn'd it into words,
But could not into one.

                   'O send away
That sad old man!' said she.   The old man went
Without a warning from his maſter's son,
Glad to escape, for sorely he now fear'd,
And the axe shone behind him in their eyes.

   HAMADRYAD.   And wouldst thou too shed the
      moſt innocent
Of blood? no vow demands it; no God wills
The oak to bleed.

   RHAICOS.   Who art thou? whence? why here?
And whither wouldſt thou go?   Among the robed
In white or saffron, or the hue that moſt
Resembles dawn or the clear sky, is none
Array'd as thou art.   What so beautiful
As that gray robe which clings about thee close,
Like moss to ſtones adhering, leaves to trees,
Yet lets thy bosom rise and fall in turn,
As, toucht by zephyrs, fall and rise the boughs
Of graceful platane by the river-side.

   HAMADRYAD.   Loveſt thou well thy father's house?
   RHAICOS.   Indeed
I love it, well I love it, yet would leave
For thine, where'er it be, my father's house,
With all the marks upon the door, that show
My growth at every birth-day since the third,
And all the charms, o'erpowering evil eyes,
My mother nail'd for me againſt my bed,
And the Cydonian bow (which thou shalt see)

Won in my race laſt spring from Eutychos.

HAMADRYAD. Bethink thee what it is to leave a home
Thou never yet haſt left, one night, one day.

RHAICOS. No, 'tis not hard to leave it; 'tis not hard
To leave, O maiden, that paternal home,
If there be one on earth whom we may love
Firſt, laſt, for ever; one who says that she
Will love for ever too.   To say which word,
Only to say it, surely is enough. . . .
It shows such kindness . . . if 'twere possible
We at the moment think she would indeed.

HAMADRYAD. Who taught thee all this folly at thy age?

RHAICOS. I have seen lovers and have learnt to love.

HAMADRYAD. But wilt thou spare the tree?

RHAICOS.   My father wants
The bark; the tree may hold its place awhile.

HAMADRYAD. Awhile! thy father numbers then my days?

RHAICOS. Are there no others where the moss beneath
Is quite as tufty?   Who would send thee forth
Or ask thee why thou tarrieſt?   Is thy flock
Anywhere near?

HAMADRYAD.   I have no flock: I kill
Nothing that breathes, that ſtirs, that feels the air,
The sun, the dew.   Why should the beautiful
(And thou art beautiful) diſturb the source
Whence springs all beauty?   Haſt thou never heard
Of Hamadryads?

RHAICOS.   Heard of them I have:

Tell me some tale about them.   May I sit
Beside thy feet?   Art thou not tired?   The herbs
Are very soft; I will not come too nigh;
Do but sit there, nor tremble so, nor doubt.
Stay, ſtay an inſtant: let me firſt explore
If any acorn of laſt year be left
Within it; thy thin robe too ill protects
Thy dainty limbs againſt the harm one small
Acorn may do.   Here's none.   Another day
Truſt me; till then let me sit opposite.

    HAMADRYAD.   I seat me; be thou seated, and con-
      tent.
    RHAICOS.   O sight for gods!   Ye men below!
      adore
The Aphroditè.   *Is* she there below?
Or sits she here before me? as she sate
Before the shepherd on those highths that shade
The Hellespont, and brought his kindred woe.

    HAMADRYAD.   Reverence the higher Powers; nor
      deem amiss
Of her who pleads to thee, and would repay . . .
Ask not how much . . . but very much.   Rise not;
No, Rhaicos, no!   Without the nuptial vow
Love is unholy.   Swear to me that none
Of mortal maids shall ever taſte thy kiss,
Then take thou mine; then take it, not before.

    RHAICOS.   Hearken, all gods above!   O Aphroditè!
O Herè! let my vow be ratified!
But wilt thou come into my father's house?

    HAMADRYAD.   Nay: and of mine I cannot give
      thee part.
    RHAICOS.   Where is it?
    HAMADRYAD.   In this oak.
    RHAICOS.   Ay; now begins

The tale of Hamadryad: tell it through.

HAMADRYAD. Pray of thy father never to cut
    down
My tree; and promise him, as well thou mayst,
That every year he shall receive from me
More honey than will buy him nine fat sheep,
More wax than he will burn to all the gods.
Why fallest thou upon thy face? Some thorn
May scratch it, rash young man! Rise up; for
    shame!

RHAICOS. For shame I cannot rise. O pity me!
I dare not sue for love . . . but do not hate!
Let me once more behold thee . . . not once more,
But many days: let me love on . . . unloved!
I aimed too high: on my head the bolt
Falls back, and pierces to the very brain.

HAMADRYAD. Go . . . rather go, than make me
    say I love.

RHAICOS. If happiness is immortality,
(And whence enjoy it else the gods above?)
I am immortal too: my vow is heard:
Hark! on the left . . . Nay, turn not from me now,
I claim my kiss.

HAMADRYAD. Do men take first, then claim?
Do thus the seasons run their course with them?

. . . Her lips were seal'd, her head sank on his breast.
'Tis said that laughs were heard within the wood:
But who should hear them? . . . and whose laughs?
    and why?
    Savoury was the smell, and long past noon,
Thallinos! in thy house; for marjoram,
Basil and mint, and thyme and rosemary,
Were sprinkled on the kid's well roasted length,

[139]

Awaiting Rhaicos. Home he came at laſt,
Not hungry, but pretending hunger keen,
With head and eyes just o'er the maple plate.
'Thou seeſt but badly, coming from the sun,
Boy Rhaicos!' said the father. 'That oak's bark
Muſt have been tough, with little sap between;
It ought to run; but it and I are old.'
Rhaicos, although each morsel of the bread
Increaſt by chewing, and the meat grew cold
And taſteless to his palate, took a draught
Of gold-bright wine, which, thirſty as he was,
He thought not of until his father fill'd
The cup, averring water was amiss,
But wine had been at all times pour'd on kid,
It was religion.
                    He thus fortified
Said, not quite boldly, and not quite abasht,
'Father, that oak is Zeusis own; that oak
Year after year will bring thee wealth from wax
And honey. There is one who fears the gods
And the gods love . . . that one.'
                              (He blusht, nor said
What one)
                'Hath promiſt this, and may do more.
We have not many moons to wait until
The bees have done their beſt: if then there come
Nor wax nor honey, let the trees be hewn.'
    'Zeus hath beſtow'd on thee a prudent mind,'
Said the glad sire: 'but look thou often there,
And gather all the honey thou canſt find
In every crevice, over and above
What hath been promiſt; would they reckon that?'
    Rhaicos went daily; but the nymph as oft
Invisible. To play at love, she knew,

Stopping its breathings when it breathes moſt soft,
Is sweeter than to play on any pipe.
She play'd on his: she fed upon his sighs;
They pleas'd her when they gently waved her hair,
Cooling the pulses of her purple veins,
And when her absence brought them out they
    pleas'd.
Even among the fondeſt of them all,
What mortal or immortal maid is more
Content with giving happiness than pain?
One day he was returning from the wood
Despondently.   She pitied him, and said
'Come back!' and twined her fingers in the hem
Above his shoulder.   Then she led his ſteps
To a cool rill that ran o'er level sand
Through lentisk and through oleander, there
Bathed she his feet, lifting them on her lap
When bathed, and drying them in both her hands.
He dared complain; for those who moſt are loved
Moſt dare it; but not harsh was his complaint.
'O thou inconſtant!' said he, 'if ſtern law
Bind thee, or will, ſtronger than ſterneſt law,
O, let me know henceforward when to hope
The fruit of love that grows for me but here.'
He spake; and pluckt it from its pliant ſtem.
'Impatient Rhaicos! why thus intercept
The answer I would give?   There is a bee
Whom I have fed, a bee who knows mv thoughts
And executes my wishes: I will send
That messenger.   If ever thou art false,
Drawn by another, own it not, but drive
My bee away: then shall I know my fate,
And, . . . for thou muſt be wretched, . . . weep at
    thine.

[141]

But often as my heart persuades to lay
Its cares on thine and throb itself to rest,
Expect her with thee, whether it be morn,
Or eve, at any time when woods are safe.'

Day after day the Hours beheld them blest
And season after season: years had past,
Blest were they still.   He who asserts that Love
Ever is sated of sweet things, the same
Sweet things he fretted for in earlier days,
Never, by Zeus! loved he a Hamadryad.
  The nights had now grown longer, and perhaps
The Hamadryads find them lone and dull
Among their woods; one did, alas!   She called
Her faithful bee: 'twas when all bees should sleep,
And all did sleep but hers.   She was sent forth
To bring that light which never wintry blast
Blows out, nor rain nor snow extinguishes,
The light that shines from loving eyes upon
Eyes that love back, till they can see no more.

Rhaicos was sitting at his father's hearth:
Between them stood the table, not o'erspread
With fruits which autumn now profusely bore,
Nor anise cakes, nor odorous wine; but there
The draft-board was expanded; at which game
Triumphant sat old Thallinos; the son
Was puzzled, vext, discomfited, distraught.
A buzz was at his ear: up went his hand,
And it was heard no longer.   The poor bee
Return'd (but not until the morn shone bright)
And found the Hamadryad with her head
Upon her aching wrist, and showed one wing
Half-broken off, the other's meshes marr'd,

And there were bruises which no eye could see
Saving a Hamadryad's.
                    At this sight
Down fell the languid brow, both hands fell down,
A shriek was carried to the ancient hall
Of Thallinos: he heard it not: his son
Heard it, and ran forthwith into the wood.
No bark was on the tree, no leaf was green,
The trunk was riven through. From that day forth
Nor word nor whisper sooth'd his ear, nor sound
Even of insect wing: but loud laments
The woodmen and the shepherds one long year
Heard day and night; for Rhaicos would not quit
The solitary place, but moan'd and died.

Hence milk and honey wonder not, O guest,
To find set duly on the hollow stone.
                              Walter Savage Landor

SONG

I

A SPIRIT haunts the year's last hours
Dwelling amid these yellowing bowers:
    To himself he talks;
For at eventide, listening earnestly,
At his work you may hear him sob and sigh
    In the walks;
    Earthward he boweth the heavy stalks
Of the mouldering flowers:
    Heavily hangs the broad sunflower
      Over its grave i' the earth so chilly;
    Heavily hangs the hollyhock,
      Heavily hangs the tigerlily.

II

The air is damp, and hushed, and close,
As a sick man's room when he taketh repose
    An hour before death;
My very heart faints and my whole soul grieves
At the moist rich smell of the rotting leaves,
    And the breath
    Of the fading edges of box beneath,
And the year's last rose.
    Heavily hangs the broad sunflower
      Over its grave i' the earth so chilly;
    Heavily hangs the hollyhock,
      Heavily hangs the tigerlily.

Alfred Tennyson

PART I

ON either side the river lie
Long fields of barley and of rye,
That clothe the wold and meet the sky;
And thro' the field the road runs by
    To many-tower'd Camelot;
And up and down the people go,
Gazing where the lilies blow
Round an island there below,
    The island of Shalott.

Willows whiten, aspens quiver,
Little breezes dusk and shiver
Thro' the wave that runs for ever
By the island in the river
    Flowing down to Camelot.
Four gray walls, and four gray towers,
Overlook a space of flowers,
And the silent isle imbowers
    The Lady of Shalott.

By the margin, willow-veil'd,
Slide the heavy barges trail'd
By slow horses; and unhail'd
The shallop flitteth silken-sail'd
    Skimming down to Camelot:
But who hath seen her wave her hand?
Or at the casement seen her stand?
Or is she known in all the land,
    The Lady of Shalott?

Only reapers, reaping early
In among the bearded barley,
Hear a song that echoes cheerly
From the river winding clearly,
     Down to tower'd Camelot:
And by the moon the reaper weary,
Piling sheaves in uplands airy,
Listening, whispers ' 'Tis the fairy
     Lady of Shalott.'

PART II

There she weaves by night and day
A magic web with colours gay.
She has heard a whisper say,
A curse is on her if she stay
     To look down to Camelot.
She knows not what the curse may **be,**
And so she weaveth steadily,
And little other care hath she,
     The Lady of Shalott.

And moving thro' a mirror clear
That hangs before her all the year,
Shadows of the world appear.
There she sees the highway near
     Winding down to Camelot:
There the river eddy whirls,
And there the surly village-churls,
And the red cloaks of market-girls,
     Pass onward from Shalott.

Sometimes a troop of damsels glad,
An abbot on an ambling pad,

Sometimes a curly shepherd-lad,
Or long-haired page in crimson clad,
　　Goes by to tower'd Camelot;
And sometimes thro' the mirror blue
The knights come riding two and two:
She hath no loyal knight and true,
　　The Lady of Shalott.

But in her web she still delights
To weave the mirror's magic sights,
For often thro' the silent nights
A funeral, with plumes and lights
　　And music, went to Camelot:
Or when the moon was overhead,
Came two young lovers lately wed;
'I am half sick of shadows,' said
　　The Lady of Shalott.

PART III

A bow-shot from her bower-eaves,
He rode between the barley sheaves,
The sun came dazzling thro' the leaves,
And flamed upon the brazen greaves
　　Of bold Sir Lancelot.
A redcross knight for ever kneel'd
To a lady in his shield,
That sparkled on the yellow field,
　　Beside remote Shalott.

The gemmy bridle glitter'd free,
Like to some branch of stars we see
Hung in the golden Galaxy.
The bridle bells rang merrily

As he rode down to Camelot:
And from his blazon'd baldric slung
A mighty silver bugle hung,
And as he rode his armour rung,
    Beside remote Shalott.

All in the blue unclouded weather
Thick-jewell'd shone the saddle-leather,
The helmet and the helmet-feather
Burn'd like one burning flame together,
    As he rode down to Camelot.
As often thro' the purple night,
Below the starry clusters bright,
Some bearded meteor, trailing light,
    Moves over still Shalott.

His broad clear brow in sunlight glow'd;
On burnish'd hooves his war-horse trode;
From underneath his helmet flowed
His coal-black curls as on he rode,
    As he rode down to Camelot.
From the bank and from the river
He flash'd into the crystal mirror,
'Tirra lirra,' by the river
    Sang Sir Lancelot.

She left the web, she left the loom,
She made three paces thro' the room,
She saw the water-lily bloom,
She saw the helmet and the plume,
    She look'd down to Camelot.
Out flew the web and floated wide;
The mirror crack'd from side to side;
'The curse is come upon me,' cried
    The Lady of Shalott.

PART IV

In the stormy east-wind straining,
The pale yellow woods were waning,
The broad stream in his banks complaining,
Heavily the low sky raining
    Over tower'd Camelot;
Down she came and found a boat
Beneath a willow left afloat,
And round about the prow she wrote
    The Lady of Shalott.

And down the river's dim expanse—
Like some bold seer in a trance,
Seeing all his own mischance—
With a glassy countenance
    Did she look to Camelot.
And at the closing of the day
She loosed the chain, and down she lay;
The broad stream bore her far away,
    The Lady of Shalott.

Lying, robed in snowy white
That loosely flew to left and right—
The leaves upon her falling light—
Thro' the noises of the night
    She floated down to Camelot:
And as the boat-head wound along
The willowy hills and fields among,
They heard her singing her last song,
    The Lady of Shalott.

Heard a carol, mournful, holy,
Chanted loudly, chanted lowly,

Till her blood was frozen slowly,
And her eyes were darken'd wholly,
    Turn'd to tower'd Camelot;
For ere she reach'd upon the tide
The first house by the water-side,
Singing in her song she died,
    The Lady of Shalott.

Under tower and balcony,
By garden-wall and gallery,
A gleaming shape she floated by,
A corse between the houses high,
    Silent into Camelot.
Out upon the wharfs they came,
Knight and burgher, lord and dame,
And round the prow they read her name,
    The Lady of Shalott.

Who is this? and what is here?
And in the lighted palace near
Died the sound of royal cheer;
And they cross'd themselves for fear,
    All the knights at Camelot;
But Lancelot mused a little space;
He said, 'She has a lovely face;
God in his mercy lend her grace,
    The Lady of Shalott.'

Alfred Tennyson

TO HELEN

HELEN, thy beauty is to me
  Like those Nicéan barks of yore
That gently, o'er a perfumed sea,
  The weary way-worn wanderer bore
  To his own native shore.

On desperate seas long wont to roam,
  Thy hyacinth hair, thy classic face,
Thy Naiad airs have brought me home
  To the glory that was Greece,
And the grandeur that was Rome.

Lo! in yon brilliant window niche
  How statue-like I see thee stand,
  The agate lamp within thy hand!
Ah, Psyche, from the regions which
  Are holy-land.

Edgar Allan Poe

ONCE it smiled, a silent dell
Where the people did not dwell;
They had gone unto the wars,
Trusting to the mild-eyed stars,
Nightly, from their azure towers,
To keep watch above the flowers,
In the midst of which all day
The red sunlight lazily lay.
Now each visitor shall confess
The sad valley's restlessness.
Nothing there is motionless—
Nothing save the airs that brood
Over the magic solitude.
Ah, by no wind are stirred those trees
That palpitate like the chill seas
Around the misty Hebrides!
Ah, by no wind those clouds are driven,
That rustle through the unquiet Heaven
Uneasily, from morn till even,
Over the violets that there lie
In myriad types of the human eye—
Over the lilies there that wave
And weep above a nameless grave!
They wave:—from out their fragrant tops
Eternal dews come down in drops.
They weep:—from off their delicate stems
Perennial tears descend in gems.

Edgar Allan Poe

DREAMLAND

BY a route obscure and lonely,
Haunted by ill angels only,
Where an Eidolon, named NIGHT,
On a black throne reigns upright,
I have reached these lands but newly
From an ultimate dim Thule—
From a wild, weird clime, that lieth sublime,
    Out of SPACE, out of Time;

Bottomless vales and boundless floods,
And chasms and caves, and Titan woods,
With forms that no man can discover
For the dews that drip all over;
Mountains toppling evermore
Into seas without a shore;
Seas that restlessly aspire,
Surging, unto skies of fire;
Lakes that endlessly outspread
Their lone waters—lone and dead,—
Their still waters—still and chilly
With the snows of the lolling lily.

By the lakes that thus outspread
Their lone waters, lone and dead,—
Their sad waters, sad and chilly
With the snows of the lolling lily,—
By the mountains—near the river,
Murmuring lowly, murmuring ever,—
By the grey woods,—by the swamp
Where the toad and the newt encamp,—
By the dismal tarns and pools
    Where dwell the Ghouls,—

By each spot the most unholy—
In each nook most melancholy,—
There the traveler meets aghast
Sheeted Memories of the Past—
Shrouded forms that start and sigh
As they pass the wanderer by—
White-robed forms of friends long given,
In agony, to the Earth—and Heaven.
For the heart whose woes are legion
'Tis a peaceful, soothing region—
For the spirit that walks in shadow
'Tis—oh, 'tis an Eldorado!
But the traveler, traveling through it,
May not—dare not openly view it;
Never its mysteries are exposed
To the weak human eye unclosed;
So wills its king, who hath forbid
The uplifting of the fringèd lid;
And thus the sad Soul that here passes
Beholds it but through darkened glasses.
By a route obscure and lonely,

Haunted by ill angels only,
Where an Eidolon, named NIGHT,
On a black throne reigns upright,
I have wandered home but newly
From this ultimate dim Thule.

Edgar Allan Poe

LO ! Death has reared himself a throne
In a strange city lying alone
Far down within the dim West,
Where the good, and the bad, and the worst, and the
      best
Have gone to their eternal rest.
There shrines and palaces and towers
(Time-eaten towers that tremble not!)
Resemble nothing that is ours.
Around, by lifting winds forgot
Resignedly beneath the sky
The melancholy waters lie.

No rays from the holy heaven come down
On the long night-time of that town;
But light from out the lurid sea
Streams up the turrets silently—
Gleams up the pinnacles far and free—
Up domes—up spires—up kingly halls—
Up fanes—up Babylon-like walls—
Up shadowy long-forgotten bowers
Of sculptured ivy and stone flowers—
Up many and many a marvellous shrine
Whose wreathèd friezes intertwine
The viol, the violet, and the vine.

Resignedly beneath the sky
The melancholy waters lie.
So blend the turrets and shadows there
That all seem pendulous in air,
While from a proud tower in the town
Death looks gigantically down.

There open fanes and gaping graves
Yawn level with the luminous waves;
But not the riches there that lie
In each idol's diamond eye—
Not the gaily-jewelled dead
Tempt the waters from their bed;
For no ripples curl, alas!
Along that wilderness of glass—
No swellings tell that winds may be
Upon some far-off happier sea—
No heavings hint that winds have been
On seas less hideously serene.

But lo, a stir is in the air!
The wave—there is a movement there!
As if the towers had thrust aside,
In slightly sinking, the dull tide—
As if their tops had feebly given
A void within the filmy Heaven.
The waves have now a redder glow—
The hours are breathing faint and low—
And when, amid no earthly moans,
Down, down that town shall settle hence
Hell, rising from a thousand thrones,
Shall do it reverence.

Edgar Allan Poe

IN the greenest of our valleys
　　By good angels tenanted,
Once a fair and stately palace—
　　Radiant palace—reared its head.
In the monarch Thought's dominion—
　　It stood there!
Never seraph spread a pinion
　　Over fabric half so fair!

Banners yellow, glorious, golden,
　　On its roof did float and flow
(This—all this—was in the olden
　　Time long ago);
And every gentle air that dallied,
　　In that sweet day,
Along the ramparts plumed and pallid,
　　A wingèd odor went away.

Wanderers in that happy valley,
　　Through two luminous windows, saw
Spirits moving musically,
　　To a lute's well-tunèd law,
Round about a throne where, sitting
　　(Porphyrogene!)
In state his glory well befitting,
　　The ruler of the realm was seen.

And all with pearl and ruby glowing
　　Was the fair palace door,
Through which came, flowing, flowing, flowing,
　　And sparkling evermore,

A troop of Echoes, whose sweet duty
    Was but to sing,
In voices of surpassing beauty,
    The wit and wisdom of their king.

But evil things, in robes of sorrow,
    Assailed the monarch's high estate.
(Ah, let us mourn!—for never morrow
    Shall dawn upon him desolate!)
And round about his home the glory
    That blushed and bloomed
Is but a dim-remembered story
    Of the old time entombed.

And travellers, now, within that valley,
    Through the red-litten windows see
Vast forms, that move fantastically
    To a discordant melody,
While, like a ghastly rapid river,
    Through the pale door
A hideous throng rush out for ever,
    And laugh—but smile no more.
                                    Edgar Allan Poe

THE skies they were ashen and sober;
 The leaves they were crispèd and sere—
 The leaves they were withering and sere;
It was night in the lonesome October
 Of my most immemorial year;
It was hard by the dim lake of Auber,
 In the misty mid region of Weir—
It was down by the dank tarn of Auber,
 In the ghoul-haunted woodland of Weir.

Here once, through an alley Titanic,
 Of cypress, I roamed with my Soul—
 Of cypress, with Psyche, my Soul.
Those were days when my heart was volcanic
 As the scoriac rivers that roll—
 As the lavas that restlessly roll
Their sulphurous currents down Yaanek
 In the ultimate climes of the pole—
That groan as they roll down Mount Yaanek
 In the realms of the boreal pole.

Our talk had been serious and sober,
 But our thoughts they were palsied and sere—
 Our memories were treacherous and sere—
For we knew not the month was October,
 And we marked not the night of the year—
 (Ah, night of all nights in the year!)
We noted not the dim lake of Auber—
 (Though once we had journeyed down here)—
Remembered not the dank tarn of Auber,
 Nor the ghoul-haunted woodland of Weir.

And now, as the night was senescent
  And star-dials pointed to morn—
  As the star-dials hinted of morn—
At the end of our path a liquescent
  And nebulous lustre was born,
Out of which a miraculous crescent
  Arose with a duplicate horn—
Astarte's bediamonded crescent
  Distinct with its duplicate horn.

And I said—'She is warmer than Dian:
  She rolls through an ether of sighs—
  She revels in a region of sighs:
She has seen that the tears are not dry on
  These cheeks, where the worm never dies,
And has come past the stars of the Lion
  To point us the path to the skies—
  To the Lethean peace of the skies—
Come up, in despite of the Lion,
  To shine on us with her bright eyes—
Come up through the lair of the Lion,
  With love in her luminous eyes.'

But Psyche, uplifting her finger,
  Said—'Sadly this star I mistrust—
  Her pallor I strangely mistrust:—
Oh, hasten!—oh, let us not linger!
  O fly!—let us fly!—for we must.'
In terror she spoke, letting sink her
  Wings until they trailed in the dust—
In agony sobbed, letting sink her
  Plumes till they trailed in the dust—
  Till they sorrowfully trailed in the dust.

I replied—'This is nothing but dreaming:
　　Let us on by this tremulous light!
　　Let us bathe in this crystalline light!
Its Sybillic splendor is beaming
　　With Hope and in Beauty to-night:—
　　See!—it flickers up the sky through the night!
Ah, we safely may trust to its gleaming,
　　And be sure it will lead us aright—
We safely may trust to a gleaming
　　That cannot but guide us aright,
　　Since it flickers up to Heaven through the night.'

Thus I pacified Psyche and kissed her,
　　And tempted her out of her gloom—
　　And conquered her scruples and gloom;
And we passed to the end of the vista,
　　But were stopped by the door of a tomb—
　　By the door of a legended tomb;
And I said—'What is written, sweet sister,
　　On the door of this legended tomb?'
　　She replied—'Ulalume—Ulalume—
　　'Tis the vault of thy lost Ulalume!'

Then my heart it grew ashen and sober
　　As the leaves that were crispèd and sere—
　　As the leaves that were withering and sere,
And I cried—'It was surely October
　　On *this* very night of last year
　　That I journeyed—I journeyed down here—
　　That I brought a dread burden down here—
　　On this night of all nights in the year,
　　Ah! what demon has tempted me here?

Well I know, now, this dim lake of Auber,
  This misty mid region of Weir—
Well I know, now, this dank tarn of Auber,
  This ghoul-haunted woodland of Weir.'
                            Edgar Allan Poe

A DIRGE

NAIAD, hid beneath the bank
  By the willowy river-side,
Where Narcissus gently sank,
  Where unmarried Echo died,
Unto thy serene repose
Waft the stricken Anterôs.

Where the tranquil swan is borne,
  Imaged in a watery glass,
Where the sprays of fresh pink thorn
  Stoop to catch the boats that pass,
Where the earliest orchis grows,
Bury thou fair Anterôs.

Glide we by, with prow and oar:
  Ripple shadows off the wave,
And reflected on the shore
  Haply play about his grave.
Folds of summer-light enclose
All that once was Anterôs.

On a flickering wave we gaze,
  Not upon his answering eyes:
Flower and bird we scarce can praise,
  Having lost his sweet replies:
Cold and mute the river flows
With our tears for Anterôs.

W. Johnson-Cory

NORTON WOOD

(DORA'S BIRTHDAY)

IN Norton Wood the sun was bright
In Norton Wood the air was light
And meek anemonies,
Kissed by the April breeze,
Were trembling left and right.
Ah, vigorous year!
Ah, primrose dear
With smile so arch!
Ah, budding larch!
Ah, hyacinth so blue,
We also must make free with you!
Where are those cowslips hiding?
But we should not be chiding—
The ground is covered every inch—
What sayest, master finch?
I see you in the swaying bough!
And very neat you are, I vow!
And Dora says it is 'the happiest day!'
Her birthday, hers!
And there's a jay,
And from that clump of firs
Shoots a great pigeon, purple, blue and gray.
And, coming home,
Well-laden, as we clomb
Sweet Walton hill,
A cuckoo shouted with a will—
'Cuckoo! cuckoo!' the first we've heard!
'Cuckoo! cuckoo!' God bless the bird!
Scarce time to take his breath,
And now 'Cuckoo!' he saith—

Cuckoo! cuckoo! three cheers!
And let the welkin ring!
He has not folded wing
Since laſt he saw Algiers.

T. E. Brown

FOR many, many days together
  The wind blew steady from the East;
For many days hot grew the weather,
  About the time of our Lady's Feast.

For many days we rode together,
  Yet met we neither friend nor foe;
Hotter and clearer grew the weather,
  Steadily did the East wind blow.

We saw the trees in the hot, bright weather,
  Clear-cut, with shadows very black,
As freely we rode on together
  With helms unlaced and bridles slack.

And often, as we rode together,
  We, looking down the green-bank'd stream,
Saw flowers in the sunny weather,
  And saw the bubble-making bream.

And in the night lay down together,
  And hung above our heads the rood,
Or watch'd night-long in the dewy weather,
  The while the moon did watch the wood.

Our spears stood bright and thick together,
  Straight out the banners stream'd behind,
As we gallop'd on in the sunny weather,
  With faces turn'd towards the wind.

Down sank our threescore spears together,
  As thick we saw the pagans ride;
His eager face in the clear fresh weather,
  Shone out that last time by my side.

Up the sweep of the bridge we dash'd together,
  It rock'd to the crash of the meeting spears,
Down rain'd the buds of the dear spring weather,
  The elm-tree flowers fell like tears.

There, as we roll'd and writhed together,
  I threw my arms above my head,
For close by my side, in the lovely weather,
  I saw him reel and fall back dead.

I and the slayer met together,
  He waited the death-stroke there in his place,
With thoughts of death in the lovely weather,
  Gapingly mazed at my madden'd face.

Madly I fought as we fought together;
  In vain: the little Christian band
The pagans drown'd, as in stormy weather,
  The river drowns low-lying land.

They bound my blood-stained hands together,
  They bound his corpse to nod by my side:
Then on we rode, in the bright March weather,
  With clash of cymbals did we ride.

We ride no more, no more together;
  My prison-bars are thick and strong,
I take no heed of any weather,
  The sweet Saints grant I live not long.
                              William Morris

THE DAMOZELS

LADY ALICE, lady Louise,
Between the wash of the tumbling seas
We are ready to sing, if so ye please;
So lay your long hands on the keys;
    Sing, *Laudate pueri.*

And ever the great bell overhead
Boom'd in the wind a knell for the dead,
Though no one toll'd it, a knell for the dead.

LADY LOUISE

Sister, let the measure swell
Not too loud; for you sing not well
If you drown the faint boom of the bell;
    He is weary, so am I.

And ever the chevron overhead
Flapp'd on the banner of the dead;
(Was he asleep, or was he dead?)

LADY ALICE

Alice the Queen, and Louise the Queen,
Two damozels wearing purple and green,
Four lone ladies dwelling here
From day to day and year to year;
And there is none to let us go;
To break the locks of the doors below,
Or shovel away the heaped-up snow;
And when we die no man will know

That we are dead; but they give us leave,
Once every year on Christmas-eve,
To sing in the Closet Blue one song;
And we should be so long, so long,
If we dared, in singing; for dream on dream,
They float on in a happy stream;
Float from the gold strings, float from the keys,
Float from the open'd lips of Louise;
But, alas! the sea-salt oozes through
The chinks of the tiles of the Closet Blue;
And ever the great bell overhead
Booms in the wind a knell for the dead,
The wind plays on it a knell for the dead.

They sing all together

How long ago was it, how long ago,
He came to this tower with hands full of snow?

Kneel down, O love Louise, kneel down! he said,
And sprinkled the dusty snow over my head.

He watch'd the snow melting, it ran through my
    hair
Ran over my shoulders, white shoulders and bare.

I cannot weep for thee, poor love Louise,
For my tears are all hidden deep under the seas;

In a gold and blue casket she keeps all my tears,
But my eyes are no longer blue, as in old years;

Yea, they grow grey with time, grow small and dry,
I am so feeble now, would I might die.

[169]

And in truth the great bell overhead
Left off his pealing for the dead,
Perchance, because the wind was dead.

Will he come back again, or is he dead?
O! is he sleeping, my scarf round his head?

Or did they strangle him as he lay there,
With the long scarlet scarf I used to wear?

Only I pray thee, Lord, let him come here!
Both his soul and his body to me are most dear.

Dear Lord, that loves me, I wait to receive
Either body or spirit this wild Christmas-eve.

Through the floor shot up a lily red,
With a patch of earth from the land of the dead,
For he was strong in the land of the dead.

What matter that his cheeks were pale,
   His kind kiss'd lips all grey?
O, love Louise, have you waited long?
   O, my lord Arthur, yea.

What if his hair that brush'd her cheek
   Was stiff with frozen rime?
His eyes were grown quite blue again,
   As in the happy time.

O, love Louise, this is the key
   Of the happy golden land!
O, sisters, cross the bridge with me,
   My eyes are full of sand.

[170]

What matter that I cannot see,
If ye take me by the hand?

And ever the great bell overhead,
And the tumbling seas mourn'd for the dead;
For their song ceased, and they were dead.
                                    William Morris

MIDWAYS of a wallèd garden,
  In the happy poplar land,
  Did an ancient castle stand,
With an old knight for a warden.

Many scarlet bricks there were
  In its walls, and old grey stone;
  Over which red apples shone
At the right time of the year.

On the bricks the green moss grew,
  Yellow lichen on the stone,
  Over which red apples shone;
Little war that castle knew.

Deep green water fill'd the moat,
  Each side had a red-brick lip,
  Green and mossy with the drip
Of dew and rain; there was a boat

Of carven wood, with hangings green
  About the stern; it was great bliss
  For lovers to sit there and kiss
In the hot summer noons, not seen.

Across the moat the fresh west wind
  In very little ripples went;
  The way the heavy aspens bent
Towards it, was a thing to mind.

The painted drawbridge over it
  Went up and down with gilded chains,
  'Twas pleasant in the summer rains
Within the bridge-house there to sit.

There were five swans that ne'er did eat
  The water-weeds, for ladies came
  Each day, and young knights did the same,
And gave them cakes and bread for meat.

They had a house of painted wood,
  A red roof gold-spiked over it,
  Wherein upon their eggs to sit
Week after week; no drop of blood,

Drawn from men's bodies by sword-blows,
  Came ever there, or any tear;
  Most certainly from year to year
'Twas pleasant as a Provence rose.

The banners seem'd quite full of ease,
  That over the turret-roofs hung down;
  The battlements could get no frown
From the flower-moulded cornices.

Who walked in that garden there?
  Miles and Giles and Isabeau,
  Tall Jehane du Castel beau,
Alice of the golden hair,

Big Sir Gervaise, the good knight,
  Fair Ellayne le Violet,
  Mary, Constance fille de fay,
Many dames with footfall light.

Whosoever wander'd there,
  Whether it be dame or knight,
  Half of scarlet, half of white
Their raiment was; of roses fair

Each wore a garland on the head,
    At Ladies' Gard the way was so.
    Fair Jehane du Castel beau
Wore her wreath till it was dead.

Little joy she had of it,
    Of the raiment white and red,
    Or the garland on her head,
She had none with whom to sit

In the carven boat at noon;
    None the more did Jehane weep,
    She would only stand and keep
Saying: He will be here soon!

Many times in the long day
    Miles and Giles and Gervaise passed,
    Holding each some white hand fast,
Every time they heard her say:

Summer cometh to an end,
    Undern cometh after noon;
    Golden wings will be here soon,
What if I some token send?

Wherefore that night within the hall,
    With open mouth and open eyes,
    Like some one listening with surprise,
She sat before the sight of all.

Stoop'd down a little she sat there,
    With neck stretch'd out and chin thrown up,
    One hand around a golden cup;
And strangely with her fingers fair

[174]

She beat some tune upon the gold;
   The minstrels in the gallery
   Sung: 'Arthur, who will never die,
In Avallon he groweth old.'

And when the song was ended, she
   Rose and caught up her gown and ran;
   None stopp'd her eager face and wan
Of all that pleasant company.

Right so within her own chamber
   Upon her bed she sat; and drew
   Her breath in quick gasps; till she knew
That no man follow'd after her.

She took the garland from her head,
   Loosed all her hair, and let it lie
   Upon the coverlet; thereby
She laid the gown of white and red;

And she took off her scarlet shoon,
   And bared her feet; still more and more
   Her sweet face redden'd; evermore
She murmur'd: 'He will be here soon;

Truly he cannot fail to know
   My tender body waits him here;
   And if he knows, I have no fear
For poor Jehane du Castel beau.'

She took a sword within her hand,
   Whose hilts were silver, and she sung
   Somehow like this, wild words that rung
A long way over the moonlit land:

Gold wings across the sea!
Grey light from tree to tree,
Gold hair beside my knee,
I pray thee come to me,
Gold wings!

            The water slips,
   The red-bill'd moorhen dips.

Sweet kisses on red lips;
Alas! the red ruſt grips,
And the blood-red dagger rips,
Yet, O knight, come to me!

Are not my blue eyes sweet?
The weſt wind from the wheat
Blows cold across my feet;
Is it not time to meet
Gold wings across the sea?

White swans on the green moat,
Small feathers left afloat
By the blue-painted boat;
Swift running of the ſtoat,
Sweet gurgling note by note
Of sweet music.

           O gold wings,
Liſten how gold hair sings,
And the Ladies' Caſtle rings,
Gold wings across the sea.

I sit on a purple bed,
Outside, the wall is red,
Thereby the apple hangs,
And the wasp, caught by the fangs,

Dies in the autumn night,
And the bat flits till light,
And the love-crazèd knight

Kisses the long wet grass:
The weary days pass,—
Gold wings across the sea.

Gold wings across the sea!
Moonlight from tree to tree,
Sweet hair laid on my knee,
O, sweet knight, come to me.

Gold wings, the short night slips,
The white swan's long neck drips,
I pray thee, kiss my lips,
Gold wings across the sea!

NO answer through the moonlit night;
   No answer in the cold grey dawn;
   No answer when the shaven lawn
Grew green, and all the roses bright.

Her tired feet look'd cold and thin,
   Her lips were twitch'd, and wretched tears,
   Some, as she lay, roll'd past her ears,
Some fell from off her quivering chin.

Her long throat, stretched to its full length,
   Rose up and fell right brokenly;
   As though the unhappy heart was nigh
Striving to break with all its strength.

And when she slipp'd from off the bed,
　　Her cramp'd feet would not hold her; she
　　Sank down and crept on hand and knee,
On the window-sill she laid her head.

There, with crooked arm upon the sill,
　　She look'd out, muttering dismally:
　　'There is no sail upon the sea,
No pennon on the empty hill.

'I cannot stay here all alone,
　　Or meet their happy faces here,
　　And wretchedly I have no fear;
A little while, and I am gone.'

Therewith she rose upon her feet,
　　And totter'd; cold and misery
　　Still made the deep sobs come, till she
At last stretch'd out her fingers sweet,

And caught the great sword in her hand;
　　And, stealing down the silent stair,
　　Barefooted in the morning air,
And only in her smock, did stand

Upright upon the green lawn grass;
　　And hope grew in her as she said:
　　'I have thrown off the white and red,
And pray God it may come to pass

'I meet him; if ten years go by
　　Before I meet him; if, indeed,
　　Meanwhile both soul and body bleed,
Yet there is end of misery,
[178]

'And I have hope.   He could not come,
    But I can go to him and show
    These new things I have got to know,
And make him speak, who has been dumb.'

O Jehane! the red morning sun
    Changed her white feet to glowing gold,
    Upon her smock, on crease and fold,
Changed that to gold which had been dun.

O Miles, and Giles, and Isabeau,
    Fair Ellayne le Violet,
    Mary, Conſtance fille de fay!
Where is Jehane du Caſtel beau?

O big Gervaise ride apace!
    Down to the hard yellow sand,
    Where the water meets the land.
This is Jehane by her face.

Why has she a broken sword?
    Mary! she is slain outright;
    Verily a piteous sight;
Take her up without a word!

Giles and Miles and Gervaise there,
    Ladies' Gard must meet the war;
    Whatsoever knights these are,
Man the walls withouten fear!

Axes to the apple-trees,
    Axes to the aspens tall!
    Barriers without the wall
May be lightly made of these.

O poor shivering Isabeau;
   Poor Ellayne le Violet,
   Bent with fear! we miss to-day
Brave Jehane du Castel beau.

O poor Mary, weeping so!
   Wretched Constance fille de fay!
   Verily we miss to-day
Fair Jehane du Castel beau.

THE apples now grow green and sour
   Upon the mouldering castle-wall,
   Before they ripen there they fall:
There are no banners on the tower,

The draggled swans most eagerly eat
   The green weeds trailing in the moat;
   Inside the rotting leaky boat
You see a slain man's stiffen'd feet.

William Morris

WHEN the hounds of Spring are on winter's traces,
  The mother of months in meadow or plain
Fills the shadows and windy places
  With lisp of leaves and ripple of rain;
And the bright brown nightingale amorous
Is half assuaged for Itylus,
For the Thracian ships and the foreign faces,
  The tongueless vigil, and all the pain.

Come with bows bent and with emptying of quivers,
  Maiden most perfect, lady of light,
With a noise of winds and many rivers,
  With a clamour of waters, and with might;
Bind on thy sandals, O thou most fleet,
Over the splendour and speed of thy feet;
For the faint east quickens, the wan west shivers,
  Round the feet of the day and the feet of the
    night.

Where shall we find her, how shall we sing to her,
  Fold our hands round her knees, and cling?
O that man's heart were as fire and could spring to
    her,
  Fire, or the strength of the streams that spring!
For the stars and the winds are unto her
As raiment, as songs of the harp-player;
For the risen stars and the fallen cling to her,
  And the southwest-wind and the west-wind sing.

For winter's rains and ruins are over,
  And all the season of snows and sins;
The days dividing lover and lover,
  The light that loses, the night that wins;

And time remembered is grief forgotten,
And frosts are slain and flowers begotten,
And in green underwood and cover
    Blossom by blossom the spring begins.

The full streams feed on flower of rushes,
    Ripe grasses trammel a travelling foot,
The faint fresh flame of the young year flushes
    From leaf to flower, and flower to fruit;
And fruit and leaf are as gold and fire,
And the oat is heard above the lyre,
And the hoofed heel of a satyr crushes
    The chestnut-husk at the chestnut root.

And Pan by noon and Bacchus by night,
    Fleeter of foot than the fleet-foot kid,
Follows with dancing and fills with delight
    The Maenad and the Bassarid;
And soft as lips that laugh and hide
The laughing leaves of the trees divide,
And screen from seeing and leave in sight
    The god pursuing, the maiden hid.

The ivy falls with the Bacchanal's hair
    Over her eyebrows hiding her eyes;
The wild vine slipping down leaves bare
    Her bright breast shortening into sighs;
The wild vine slips with the weight of its leaves,
But the berried ivy catches and cleaves
To the limbs that glitter, the feet that scare
    The wolf that follows, the fawn that flies.

Algernon Charles Swinburne

THE END

INDEX OF POEMS

[184]